Closing the Inclusion Gap

Special and Mainstream Schools Working in Partnership

Rita Cheminais

 David Fulton Publishers

David Fulton Publishers Ltd
The Chiswick Centre, 414 Chiswick High Road, London W4 5TF

www.fultonpublishers.co.uk

First published in Great Britain by David Fulton Publishers 2003

10 9 8 7 6 5 4 3 2

David Fulton Publishers is a division of Granada Learning, part of Granada plc.

British Library Cataloguing in Publication Data
A catalogue record for this book is available from the British Library.

ISBN 1-84312-085-2

Typeset by Kenneth Burnley, Wirral, Cheshire
Printed in the UK by The Thanet Press, Margate.

Contents

Acknowledgements   v
Abbreviations   vii
Introduction   ix

Chapter 1
Redefining the future role of the special school   1
The national perspective on the future role of the special school 2
Inclusive schooling and children with SEN   3
The challenge for special schools   4
What is 'special' about special schools?   4
How to develop inclusive mainstream links   5
Valuable experiences special school leaders can share with
    mainstream partners   6
Key factors in working together   8
Identifying potential mainstream partners   8
Outcomes   11
Inclusion indicators   11
Features of inclusive special schools   12
Successful management   12
Effectiveness   12

Chapter 2
Preparing for a changing role   15
Action planning   16
Marketing   16
Marketing tips   18
Developing staff inclusion roles   21
Consultancy and outreach role   22
Coaching   23
Team building   24
Problem-solving   25
Communication   25
Stress management   26

Chapter 3
Enhancing mainstream school capacity to become more inclusive   31
Key partnership factors   32
Factors enhancing access   34
What mainstream can offer special schools   34
Inhibitors to inclusion partnerships   35
Receiving special school staff/pupils   35
Inclusion contracts   36
Mainstream training   36
Core SEN specialist standards   42
Managing dual placements   44

Chapter 4
Quality first inclusion partnerships   51
Clusters   52
Networks   52
Inclusive learning communities   53
Benefits and outcomes   54
Principles of monitoring and evaluation   55
How to monitor SEN and inclusion   56
Governors' monitoring role   56
LEAs monitoring and evaluating SEN and inclusion   70
LEA inclusion strategy   71

Appendices
Appendix 1: Inclusive learning services marketing brochure   75
Appendix 2: Inclusion service level agreement   79
Appendix 3: Inclusion service client satisfaction survey   81
Appendix 4: Example of a special school inclusion open day programme 83
Appendix 5: Parents' and carers' guide to dual placements   85
Appendix 6: The teachers' professional learning framework   89

References and further reading   93

Index   95

Acknowledgements

My interest in developing inclusive educational partnerships between special and mainstream schools arose from my work as General Adviser for SEN in Tameside LEA during 1999–2002, and as Senior SEN Adviser in Cheshire County Council during 2003.

In preparing this third book on inclusion, I sought the views and experiences of Senior Managers working in special and mainstream schools. I am appreciative of the key factors they identified as being crucial to developing and sustaining productive partnerships between the two school sectors.

I am deeply indebted to my colleagues in the Inclusion and School Improvement Service (ISIS) in Cheshire County Council, who have continued to promote diversity and educational inclusion within a framework of school improvement.

I am grateful to Maggie Atkinson, County Manager for ISIS, and also to Denis Taylor, Principal Adviser, for giving me the opportunity to disseminate my knowledge and expertise on inclusion to other interested and committed educational professionals and practitioners nationally.

My thanks go to my colleagues Allen Bowen and Mike O'Connor, both Senior SEN Advisers in Cheshire County Council, for their loyal support and encouragement in enabling me to produce this sequel to my two earlier publications entitled *Developing Inclusive School Practice* and *Inclusion and School Improvement.*

I am grateful to colleagues at the Centre for Special Education, University College Worcester, especially Joe Hodgson; and to Zita McCormick, SEN Advisory Team Leader in Hertfordshire County Council, for their continuing interest, support and valued comments regarding my publications.

I wish to thank my family and friends for their patience and endurance in supporting me during the writing of this book. In particular, Philip Eastwood Advanced Skills Teacher (AST) for Initial Teacher Training (ITT) who continues to inspire and convince me that the books I produce will make a difference to improving inclusive school policy and practice.

As always, the staff at David Fulton Publishers have helped to keep me on schedule in my writing, and their constructive guidance has been greatly valued.

While every effort has been made to acknowledge sources throughout the book, such is the range of inclusion aspects covered, however, that I may have unintentionally omitted to mention their origin. If so, I offer my apologies to all concerned.

RITA CHEMINAIS

Abbreviations

ADHD	Attention Deficit Hyperactivity Disorder
AEN	Additional Educational Needs
AST	Advanced Skills Teacher
BESD	Behavioural, Emotional and Social Difficulties
CIM	Chartered Institute of Marketing
CPD	Continuing Professional Development
CSIE	Centre for Studies on Inclusive Education
DDA	Disability Discrimination Act
DfEE	Department for Education and Employment
DfES	Department for Education and Skills
EBD	Emotional and Behavioural Difficulties
GTC	General Teaching Council
HE	Higher Education
HMI	Her Majesty's Inspector
ICT	Information and Communications Technology
IEP	Individual Education Plan
ILP	Inclusive Learning Plan
INCO	Inclusion Coordinator
INSET	In-service Education and Training
IQM	Inclusion Quality Mark
ISIS	Inclusion and School Improvement Service
IT	Information Technology
ITT	Initial Teacher Training
KS	Key Stage
LEA	Local Education Authority
LGR	Local Government Reform
LSA	Learning Support Assistant
NC	National Curriculum
NCSL	National College for School Leadership
NLNS	National Literacy and Numeracy Strategies
NPBEA	National Policy Board for Educational Administration
NQT	Newly Qualified Teacher
OFSTED	Office for Standards in Education
PLASC	Pupil Level Annual School Census
PMT	Performance Management Threshold
PoS	Programmes of Study
PRU	Pupil Referral Unit
PSHE	Personal, Social and Health Education

PSHCE	Personal, Social, Health and Citizenship Education
QCA	Qualifications and Curriculum Authority
SALT	Speech and Language Therapist
SEN	Special Educational Needs
SENCO	Special Educational Needs Coordinator
SENDA	Special Educational Needs and Disability Act
SLA	Service Level Agreement
SMSC	Spiritual, Moral, Social and Cultural
SoW	Schemes of Work
SULP	Social Use of Language Programme
TA	Teaching Assistant
TPLF	Teachers' Professional Learning Framework
TTA	Teacher Training Association
VAK	Visual, Auditory and Kinaesthetic

Introduction

The inclusion partnership dilemma

My role as adviser for special educational needs involves challenging and supporting mainstream and special schools to improve their inclusive practice. Since taking on this role, it has become evident that, while senior managers, inclusion coordinators (INCOs) and special educational needs coordinators (SENCOs) may have the 'will' to become more inclusive, there is a lack of practical guidance at national and local level on how these schools can promote productive partnerships. There also exists the dichotomy between measuring educational outcomes in terms of narrowly focused examination and test results, and including in mainstream schools children whose achievements are not recognised in national school performance tables.

Accompanying this dilemma are the ambiguity, contradiction and confusion surrounding the national inclusion strategy. On the one hand there is the drive to promote more inclusive mainstream practice, while at the same time there remains the option of retaining separate special school provision, for a minority group who remain segregated.

The central task in developing more inclusive educational practice involves the refocusing of the role of the special school, the transfer of specialist resources to mainstream settings, and the restructuring of mainstream schools to increase their capacity to respond to greater pupil diversity. An inclusive school can be defined as one in which all children and young people in the community have the opportunity to learn together.

Sir Andrew Foster, Controller of the Audit Commission, stated: '. . . We need to build schools' capacity to respond to the wide range of children's needs in classrooms today. Increasing teachers' skills and confidence is a priority' (2002a).

Removing barriers to learning, and developing appropriate strategies which enable quality teaching to occur, are central to inclusive schooling. Inclusion, as a long-term challenge, is about inclusive learning and learners' requirements, rather than *where* a child or young person is educated. Inclusion is about the ability of any school to offer appropriate curriculum access and support arrangements, as well as effective pupil management systems. It is a known fact that pupils do not make optimum progress when they are treated uniformly.

If the national goal for inclusion is to continue to reduce the number of children being educated in segregated special provision, then there has to be a planned programme of staff development, increased outreach support and guidance to mainstream schools, and a robust monitoring system in place, which will evaluate the impact of inclusive education on the attainment and progress of all pupils. This book outlines how this might be achieved.

Some educationalists may argue that as long as full-time placements exist at special schools, mainstream schools can retain the option not to change their practice, and organisations not to become more inclusive. It also restricts more specialist resources being redistributed to mainstream settings in order to facilitate more inclusive practice.

Partnership arrangements between mainstream and special schools that promote inclusive practice need to be dynamic and organic in order to enable children to move between the two settings, according to their needs. This type of practice requires flexible, responsive funding arrangements and creative resource management between partnership schools.

Special schools need to be viewed as part of a progression towards inclusion; part of the inclusion community – acting as 'launch pads' for the delivery of more flexible and effective advice and support to mainstream schools.

Inclusive partnerships

Inclusive partnerships between mainstream and special schools are likely to have a number of implications for senior staff, requiring them to:

- undertake regular self-review of inclusive policy and practice, using such audit tools as the Index for Inclusion, the Inclusion Quality Mark, and the OFSTED self-evaluation schedule for evaluating educational inclusion;

- pool funding to allow for a greater exchange of staff expertise and specialist resources, between settings, to accommodate pupil diversity;

- provide a planned, ongoing programme of joint continuing professional development for teachers and support staff from both schools;

- ensure inclusion is a priority and features on the schools' improvement plans;

- ensure that good quality induction procedures are in place to prepare special school pupils for their transition and placement in mainstream schools;

- ensure that mainstream pupils and staff are fully informed and prepared for meeting the needs of special school pupils being included;

- check that transport arrangements allow for special school children and young people to engage in out-of-hours learning activities alongside their mainstream peers;

- keep parents, governors and the local community fully informed about the inclusion activities and achievements of pupils within the partnership via regular media coverage, school newsletters, the school website or inclusion open days;

- check that flexible timetabling arrangements can be accommodated between schools to allow for joint curriculum planning and inclusion activities.

The aim of this book

The aim of this book is to enable all those involved in inclusive partnerships to know:

- what their role and expectations are;
- how to action plan for proposed inclusion activities;
- how to develop joint practice, initiatives and projects by innovating and risk-taking;
- what aspects of inclusion training are essential for staff and pupils in both settings;
- how best to disseminate good practice related to inclusion;
- how to cluster and collaborate effectively; and
- how to evaluate and monitor the impact of inclusive policy and practice within the partnership.

Who the book is for

- Head teachers and senior managers in special and mainstream schools and FE colleges.
- Inclusion coordinators and SENCOs.
- LEA school improvement officers, advisers, inspectors and inclusion consultants.
- Educational psychologists.
- Senior education lecturers in higher education.
- Governors with responsibility for SEN and inclusion.

How the format is designed to be used

- To act as a point of quick reference to senior managers, INCOs and SENCOs.
- To enable pages to be photocopied for developmental purposes, within the purchasing institution.
- There is an accompanying CD which allows readers to download and amend templates on their computers.

Redefining the future role of the special school

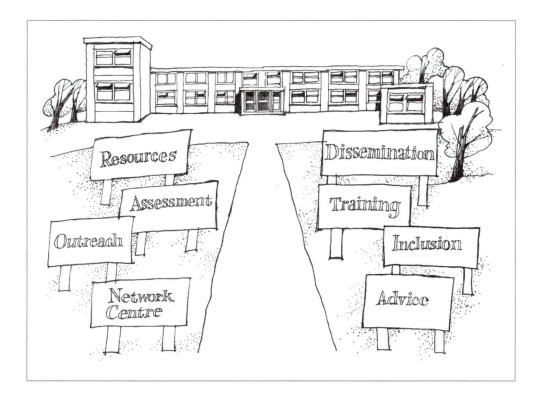

The national perspective on the future role of the special school

The DfEE Green Paper (1997) recognised that the context in which special schools were operating had changed. Their pupil populations were becoming more diverse and complex in relation to the types of special needs and the range of ability, placing increasing pressure on special schools to deal with a wider spectrum of needs.

It was considered that special schools would need to work more closely with support services, as well as with, and alongside, mainstream schools. The Green Paper also expressed the rather simplistic view that teachers in special schools were uniquely equipped to help their colleagues in mainstream schools to provide for pupils with more complex and diverse needs.

There was recognition that there would be resource implications, not least in the training which some special school teachers would require, in order to support capacity-building in mainstream schools.

Building on existing good practice was recommended as a way forward, particularly in relation to:

- cooperative working;
- shared facilities;
- shared teaching and non-teaching expertise;
- special schools becoming part of mainstream school cluster arrangements;
- special schools setting targets for the amount of 'inclusion time' pupils should spend in mainstream settings;
- more flexible pupil placements being on offer, i.e. some full-time, others part-time or short-term;
- special school staff supporting some children in mainstream placements;
- helping mainstream schools to implement inclusion policies;
- providing a source of training and advice for mainstream colleagues;
- co-location of special schools on the same site with mainstream schools to create larger learning campuses, with opportunities for interchange between staff and pupils;
- special school staff refocusing their work in resourced mainstream schools.

In 1998 the DfEE, in its *Programme of Action*, stressed that there would be a continuing role for specialist provision, including special schools:

> Special schools need to be confident, outward-looking centres of excellence. We want to build on their strengths and ensure that they are an integral part of an inclusive education system for children in their area. (DfEE 1998: 12)

Special schools were no longer being viewed as settings where pupils had to spend their entire school careers.

In 1999, Ainscow *et al.*, in a DfEE research report which focused on special and mainstream schools working together, identified a positive role for special schools and services in supporting the deep changes in attitudes and practices required to move towards greater inclusion. It was considered that this would be achieved largely by the sharing of complementary expertise and resources, with professional development being a two-way exchange process.

The report did, however, acknowledge the difficulties associated with special schools supporting mainstream school capacity-building:

- pupils remaining in the special school setting could be disadvantaged by the most effective special school staff spending time in the mainstream school at the expense of teaching time;
- some special school teachers may experience deskilling when faced with unfamiliar mainstream systems and practices;
- some special school class teachers may experience role conflict and tension when working in an in-class support capacity within a mainstream classroom;
- curriculum coverage may be limited due to a lack of specialist resources/facilities and insufficient staff subject expertise;
- some teachers may lack confidence in adopting an 'advisory' role.

Clearly, the future of the special schools is dependent on their willingness to work in closer collaboration with mainstream schools, and to complement rather than duplicate the work of delegated support services. They will need to establish outreach work, as well as offering resources and consultancy, and market themselves as a 'service'.

Inclusive schooling and children with SEN

In 2001, the DfES defined inclusion as being:

> . . . about engendering a sense of community and belonging and encouraging mainstream and special schools and others to come together to support each other and pupils with special educational needs. (DfES 2001a: para. 8)

The DfES (2001) recognised that special schools would have a continuing and vital role to play within an inclusive education system, working with their mainstream partners and other special schools. Inclusion would have to be operationalised to incorporate specialism.

Dual placements were referred to as supporting inclusion. This is where a child attends both a special school and a mainstream school. A dual-registered child, deemed to be educated at a mainstream school, must spend 51 per cent or more of his or her time there.

The annual report of the Chief HMI 2001–2 noted:

> Special schools are playing their part in the move towards increased inclusion in the mainstream by rebuilding links with mainstream schools, which have sometimes been lost in recent years. The links are providing valuable experiences for special school pupils and are broadening the horizons of pupils and staff. A number of special schools with beacon status have made joint working with mainstream schools a specific focus of their enhanced role, with pupils and staff moving both ways between schools. As funding is further delegated to schools, the funding and management of inclusion initiatives is becoming more school based. (OFSTED 2003a: 271)

The DfES Report of the Special Schools Working Group states:

> Special schools have a vast wealth of knowledge, skills and experience which, if harnessed, unlocked and effectively utilised by mainstream schools, can help ensure that inclusion is a success. (DfES 2003b: 6)

The SEN Action Programme advocates 'developing a clear future role for special schools working in partnership with mainstream schools as part of an inclusive education system' (DfES 2003a: 2).

The challenge for special schools

The challenge for special schools will be immense in relation to undertaking these new roles. Clearly, there will need to be a reappraisal of the skills and competences of staff in special schools to see how far these can be applied to mainstream settings. It also requires careful planning of appropriate ways for these special school staff to teach their mainstream counterparts. It is also reliant on mainstream teachers being ready and receptive to changes in their current practice.

As inclusion becomes accepted standard practice, special school head teachers are likely to become managers of services. Special schools are likely to evolve as specialist learning centres working flexibly with a group of schools in supporting pupils and staff in becoming more inclusive. The concept of the 'full service school' with multi-disciplinary teams (including health and social services professionals) providing a coordinated package to 'the client', working in a holistic way and on the same site, is the ideal practice for facilitating inclusion.

What is 'special' about special schools?

In response to the question 'What is special about special schools and special teaching?' supporters of responsible inclusion consider that there is nothing special or unique about either. Good inclusive practice in any school setting is reliant on high quality, multi-sensory teaching that facilitates pupils' learning in their preferred learning style.

The Audit Commission's report on SEN raised some interesting issues in relation to special school teachers' expertise:

> Although special school staff may have much experience in working with children with particular needs, many have had little specific training. Special schools tend to recruit generalists and train them once in post, reflecting the lack of training courses for special school teachers nationally. (Audit Commission 2002a: 102)

> Special school staff are on average older than their mainstream counterparts, with a significant proportion nearing retirement, and few young staff are joining to replace them. This raises serious concern about the sustainability of the special sector and the quality of the provision within it, at a time when the needs of special school pupils are becoming increasingly complex and diverse. (Audit Commission 2002a: 103)

As a higher degree of inclusion is achieved, and teachers move between main-stream and special schools, there will be increased opportunities for mainstream staff to develop more specialist skills. With increased confidence they may also be more inclined to apply for posts in special settings, so resolving some of the recruitment difficulties.

There is recognition, however, of the important work done by special schools and an acknowledgement of the continuing significant role they will play in the foreseeable future, in the spectrum of SEN provision.

The DfEs, in their report of the Special Schools Working Group, outlines what makes special schools special, unique and valued:

- the ability to offer a differentiated learning environment;
- a place where a child can feel the same as his/her peers, rather than feeling different;
- using teaching methods such as Social Use of Language Programme (SULP) and Living Language;
- the utilisation of the sophistication of staff skills to engage a child in the curriculum;
- alternative teaching strategies and specialist interventions;
- teaching to objectives;
- utilising a multi-agency approach;
- recognition of the child's affective domain, e.g. dignity, confidence and emotional well-being;
- measuring progress in mobility or independence against IEP targets.
  (DfES 2003b: 108, para. 6)

One size will never fit all. As long as diversity of need exists, there will always be a requirement for a diversity of provision. Inclusion does not necessitate main-streaming all pupils, and cannot mean the end of all special schools. A pragmatic approach to inclusion supports the notion that there is always likely to be a minority of pupils with severe and complex needs requiring specialised support in specialist settings.

How to develop inclusive mainstream links

School partnerships are a two-way exchange process, whereby both parties work collaboratively for the mutual benefit of the children. Participants are likely to ask the initial question 'What's in it for us?'. If the advantages of partnership working are not made explicit from the start, then sustaining productive links will be problematic.

The SEN *Code of Practice* comments:

Partnerships can only work when there is a clear understanding of the respective aims, roles and responsibilities of the partners and the nature of their relationships, which in turn depends on clarity of information, good communication and transparent policies. (DfES 2001b: 1.7)

Partnership based on commitment and responsibility must be central to the development of inclusive practice. For a partnership to work successfully both sides need to be clear about what they are seeking from it. Having an inclusion policy that makes this explicit is helpful. Whether schools come together is fundamentally down to the attitude and determination of the head teacher, staff and governors.

It is essential to be clear and 'up front' about what each school wants to get out of the relationship and how much time and resources they can commit. Partnerships can break down quickly when just one school does not dedicate enough time to making it work.

'Partnership' is the current buzzword for special schools, and mainstream school head teachers have much to learn from special school colleagues. To successfully work with and establish positive relationships with mainstream schools, special school head teachers need to understand mainstream limitations and constraints (such as the complexity of timetabling).

Partnerships between mainstream and special schools enable both to:

- offer greater support and diversity to all pupils;
- enable children in mainstream to learn new skills, e.g. signing for the deaf, and develop greater awareness and understanding of diverse needs;
- share creativity, risk, responsibility and resources;
- be more effective in curriculum delivery;
- attract more and different funding;
- develop non-hierarchical styles of working and distributed leadership;
- make more effective use of teaching assistants.

Valuable experiences special school leaders can share with mainstream partners

- Multi-tasking, as they often have fewer senior and middle managers, compared to mainstream schools.
- Managing more than one initiative, with fewer staff and a narrower spread of expertise – especially in a 2–19 age range school that caters for a wide spectrum of needs.
- Have experience of an external leadership role, e.g. acting as a consultant to inform the LEA's inclusion policy-making and contribute to its professional development programme.
- Sharing power and working collaboratively and cooperatively with school staff, and those from other agencies, adopting a community approach to leadership.
- Working in partnership and developing closer bonds with parents, carers and families.
- Having more direct contact with learners and staff.
- Focusing on transformation, i.e. on the empowerment for learners.
- Being creative, especially in adapting mainstream guidance for the special school context.
- Being confident, flexible, versatile decision-makers and problem-solvers, within their own sector and across agency boundaries.
- Addressing more of their own professional development needs, often because relevant professional development opportunities are not provided for them locally. (NCSL 2003: 26–7)

Leaders of special schools are quite clearly an important part of inclusion. In the context of inclusion and school improvement, the role of the special school must be about extending the curriculum, creating flexibility and developing a climate for learning. Special school leaders must use their networking skills to go out and build partnerships. The most innovative special school leaders use national initiatives like the Specialist School Programme to build expertise and links with mainstream. Their leaders spend considerable time developing and facilitating professional development opportunities, running training and creatively adapting resources and curriculum materials through expertise rooted firmly in practice. Government guidance, policy and infrastructure has not particularly recognised this expertise, when developing mainstream inclusive practice. It is time, however, to correct this oversight and create avenues for the sharing of expert knowledge and skills with mainstream staff.

Special schools are now acquiring greater confidence in their strengths and skills in relation to inclusion. This has to be followed up with a well-articulated description of what special schools have to offer – possibly a menu outlining the range of 'services' and opportunities on offer to their mainstream counterparts.

Inclusive Schooling: Children with Special Educational Needs (DfES 2001a) gave examples of how special schools could support inclusion. These included:

- providing an outreach programme to mainstream schools to enable the inclusion of a child with SEN;
- providing assessment of children's needs;
- providing training to mainstream teachers, SENCOs, teaching assistants, lunchtime supervisors, and the child's parents;
- providing support and advice to mainstream schools and other professionals;
- developing a school inclusion team;
- sharing resources and best practice with local mainstream schools;
- engaging in joint activities, initiatives, projects and social events with mainstream partners;
- establishing an Inclusion Forum to provide opportunities for support and networking across the county and within an area cluster;
- producing guidance booklets for teachers, teaching assistants, parents and pupils;
- producing videos for training purposes on inclusion;
- establishing a school web page on inclusion, which would link to other national websites.

The 'drivers' of inclusion partnerships have to be the senior managers within the special school and they will need to make out a convincing case to their mainstream colleagues in order to make the partnership attractive.

There are several methods of developing initial links with mainstream schools, though some element of risk-taking and innovation are likely to be essential factors in the process, on both sides of the partnership.

Key factors in working together

- Ensure partner schools agree a shared focus and purpose for working together.
- Tap into the leadership potential of all staff.
- Share knowledge about what is working, with other schools, and publicise and share inclusion successes through newsletters, a website, reports, brochures, INSET and networks.
- Forge partnerships with HE institutions, LEAs and external consultants.
- Develop a resource bank to use within and across schools.
- Document the partnership process.
- Plan for the long term and recognise the potential for resource sharing, training and administration.

There remains a certain amount of 'unintentional' ignorance on the part of mainstream school staff about what good inclusive learning actually looks like in special schools. This situation has not been addressed by the special schools themselves (with the exception of beacon schools) because they have continued to consider themselves to be on the periphery of education and their good practice seemed 'irrelevant' to mainstream settings.

However, if mainstream staff can see the special school in action, and observe effective classroom strategies – many of which do not require a great deal of specialist SEN knowledge or expensive resources – they are more likely to accept these children into their classrooms and feel more confident about inclusion.

Changing the mind-set and attitudes of mainstream colleagues towards SEN and disability is an aspect of inclusion that requires a continued focus, especially in relation to raising awareness about what special school children can and do achieve.

Identifying potential mainstream partners

There are likely to be 'natural' mainstream partners, i.e. those neighbourhood schools either nearby, or co-located with the special school, where some informal links already occur. Alternatively, there may be new prospective mainstream partners to approach, who may have particular subject specialisms or 'state of the art' subject facilities which would benefit special school pupils, as members of the local community.

Checklist for identifying possible mainstream partners

Within the school or setting, there is:

- a positive school culture and ethos relating to inclusion;
- good leadership and management from the head teacher and senior staff;
- an effective SENCO and/or inclusion co-ordinator;
- a good communication system that extends to parents, external agencies and members of the local community;
- a willingness to admit children with special needs;
- some history of success in including children with more complex needs;
- recognition and celebration of achievement for pupils with SEN;

Box 1.1	**Examples of how special schools can develop mainstream partnerships**

- Publicise the special school inclusion menu via a promotional leaflet, with an accompanying head teacher letter, to all local mainstream schools, inviting interest.

- Negotiate with LEA advisers or consultants to join in any summer or Easter school programmes with mainstream schools, and in return provide additional teaching assistant and teacher support from the special school staff during the event.

- Put forward a cross-curriculum project proposal, e.g. a theme: 'metamorphosis', and invite mainstream staff and pupils to participate either in the special school setting, or on neutral ground, e.g. FE college, professional development centre, specialist or beacon school.

- Advertise the desire to establish mainstream inclusion links in the local LEA SEN or inclusion Newsletter, which is distributed to all schools.

- Seek sponsorship from a local business, sports club or voluntary organisation, to run a joint activity with a receptive mainstream school.

- Participate in a national or local Inclusion Week, and publicise the events on the CSIE or LEA inclusion website.

- Combine with a mainstream school to work on preparing a joint bid for specialist school/advanced school status, which will ensure that the special school benefits from the specialist expertise and facilities within the mainstream setting.

- Utilise established LEA networks for head teachers, deputy head teachers, SENCOs, to invite interest from mainstream schools, in establishing an inclusion partnership activity or event.

- Offer to pool together or match-fund national strategy resources with a mainstream school, in order to help them meet the needs of a cohort of SEN children, functioning below or at the lower NC levels.

- Send out a video illustrating edited highlights of aspects of special school celebration activities and/or achievements of children to the head teachers of mainstream schools (particularly those serving the catchment areas of pupils at special school), and request in return one memorable 'fun' learning opportunity in the summer term, after examinations and tests are completed.

- Hold an open day at the special school, inviting head teachers, SENCOs, INCOs, subject leaders/coordinators from mainstream schools to view the school in operation, and to participate in some of the day's activities. This could entail demonstration lessons, workshop sessions, drama and dance performances, pupils producing refreshments, printing the programmes, or making a video or multi-media presentation of the day's events for the school website.

- Establish an e-mail 'pupil buddy scheme' between the mainstream and specialist school.

- an appreciation of external support and existing partnership links;
- a school development plan that has inclusion as a priority;
- a willingness by staff to improve inclusive practice within the classroom.

The special school should not be seen as a 'rescue service' or as a 'quick fix' to resolving long-term SEN issues within a school in challenging circumstances. The LEA will already be providing additional support and resources in such situations. However, the special school may be requested by the LEA to focus on a particular aspect of SEN, and complement the work of other agencies or 'fill a gap' in provision.

Whatever the circumstances, partnerships have to be built on a relationship of trust, and not viewed totally as a one-way process. Once a partnership arrangement is established, and mainstream teachers begin to feel more confident, and demonstrate the capacity and skills to deliver effective inclusive practice themselves, then the special school can start to withdraw some or all of its support and intervention.

There should be an expectation that the mainstream school staff and pupils will have the opportunity to work and socialise in the special school setting. 'Buddy' schemes for staff and SEN pupils between special and mainstream schools produce productive support and 'self-help' networks, and can result in some interesting and innovative 'spin-offs'.

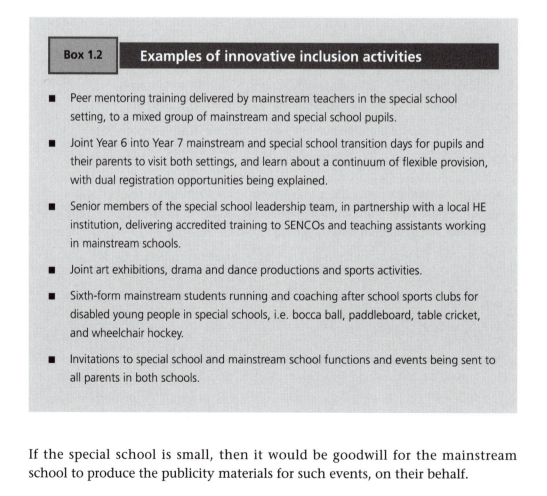

| Box 1.2 | **Examples of innovative inclusion activities** |

- Peer mentoring training delivered by mainstream teachers in the special school setting, to a mixed group of mainstream and special school pupils.

- Joint Year 6 into Year 7 mainstream and special school transition days for pupils and their parents to visit both settings, and learn about a continuum of flexible provision, with dual registration opportunities being explained.

- Senior members of the special school leadership team, in partnership with a local HE institution, delivering accredited training to SENCOs and teaching assistants working in mainstream schools.

- Joint art exhibitions, drama and dance productions and sports activities.

- Sixth-form mainstream students running and coaching after school sports clubs for disabled young people in special schools, i.e. bocca ball, paddleboard, table cricket, and wheelchair hockey.

- Invitations to special school and mainstream school functions and events being sent to all parents in both schools.

If the special school is small, then it would be goodwill for the mainstream school to produce the publicity materials for such events, on their behalf.

Outcomes

Traditionally, special schools have focused on inputs and processes, and how pupils as individuals learn best, while mainstream schools have been concerned with outcomes in the form of academic results as expressed in league tables.

The lack of national benchmarks, i.e. expected standards of achievement for children with learning difficulties, has made it difficult to assess whether a child with SEN is making reasonable progress, and to set suitably challenging targets. The Pupil Level Annual Schools Census (PLASC) collects information electronically on the performance of individual SEN pupils however, allowing for their progress to be tracked. This system of data capture, which incorporates 'P' levels, should eventually enable meaningful benchmarks to be developed.

The government is also keen to explore ways in which pupils' achievements can be recognised, other than through academic data. Suggestions include recording progress in relation to key life skills such as communication skills, problem-solving, citizenship and aspects of Personal, Social and Health Education (PSHE). This may start to address the issue of measuring the outcomes of inclusive practice and co-placement of pupils at special and mainstream schools.

It is becoming apparent that when evaluating inclusive practices, it is more appropriate to examine the effectiveness of particular aspects of inclusion. There is still a need to continue to focus on the experiences and outcomes of inclusion, in an attempt to identify causal relationships, examining the strengths and relative impacts of a range of factors, together with qualitative experiences of participants in the process, i.e. staff and pupils.

Inclusion indicators

The DfES inclusion indicators monitor how effectively special and mainstream schools are contributing to the government's inclusion agenda. The indicators look at how successfully pupils are being included or re-integrated into mainstream schools. They also consider the range of work undertaken by special schools, in partnership with mainstream schools in overcoming barriers to learning and inclusion within mainstream settings.

The process for setting inclusion indicators and monitoring progress against them involves:

- each school setting inclusion indicators at the start of the school year, which are set out in the school's SEN policy statement;
- the school outlining how it intends to meet the inclusion indicators in its annual reports to parents, and the school prospectus;
- OFSTED inspectors monitoring the school's performance against the inclusion indicators set, as well as evaluating how well the school is implementing its inclusion strategies.

Schools that have a good track record of achieving against their inclusion indicators will be eligible to receive an inclusion quality mark, tailored to suit local contexts, accredited by a Higher Education institution, and validated by the LEA. OFSTED school inspection judgements regarding inclusion are also likely to be put on a par with academic achievement. Similarly, the DfES would be well advised to establish the quality of a school's inclusivity as a key criterion in assessing their eligibility and recognition for national awards and initiatives, such as advanced schools, specialist schools, beacon school status.

Features of inclusive special schools

The government suggests how special schools can take more of a central role in the development of inclusive practices. In addition to the features previously mentioned, such as providing direct pupil support, advising mainstream colleagues, sharing facilities, resources, teaching and non-teaching expertise, and joining mainstream clusters, they add:

- building on their strengths to ensure the special school becomes an integral part of an inclusive education system;
- allowing greater flexibility on admitting pupils by taking pupils for shorter periods of time to meet specific short-term needs;
- providing quality time for special school staff to plan support with mainstream colleagues, prior to placement for pupils who could benefit from a mainstream setting;
- providing staff to work in resourced schools or units in mainstream schools;
- amalgamating small special schools and encouraging them to work as part of a larger mainstream campus, i.e. a federation or academy of schools.

Successful management

The Chief HMI in his OFSTED report 2001–2 made reference to the characteristics of excellent management in special schools, which relates closely to mainstream settings, in the promotion of inclusion. These characteristics were:

- The implementation and monitoring of whole school approaches to functions such as assessment and the recording of progress.
- The management of change, particularly the implementation of inclusion policies that bring a new and extended role for the school.
- Promoting the school's successful adjustment to dealing with a wider range of special needs. (OFSTED 2003a, para. 252)

Teamwork, the creation of vision, accountability, influence and distributed leadership are clearly relevant to successful change management, in enabling special schools to move forward in developing their new roles.

Effectiveness

It is acknowledged that effective inclusive schools require clear inclusion policies, good administrative leadership and ongoing professional development for staff. Effectiveness is a relative concept, and schools can demonstrate varying degrees of effective inclusive practice. For example, schools may be effective in promoting only a narrow range of inclusion outcomes, for a particular group of SEN pupils, as opposed to the broader continuum, over a given period of time. Lipsky and Gardner (1996) and Wang *et al.* (1998), in Campbell (2002) identified key factors necessary for inclusion to be successful:

- visionary leadership;
- collaboration – and the inclusion of all stakeholders;
- negotiated written agreements that clarify roles, aims and procedures;
- refocused use of assessment;
- support for staff and pupils;
- ongoing continuing professional development;
- stable and sufficient funding;
- parent education and parental involvement;
- ample time given for planning links;
- school readiness to include;
- SEN children's readiness for a mainstream experience;
- inclusive curriculum access, adaptation and programmes;
- adoption of inclusive teaching and learning approaches;
- effective coordination of inter-agency service provision.

Fullan (2002) regards the following essential components as being valid to special schools, in creating a collaborative culture with mainstream schools:

- building on expertise;
- pooling resources;
- providing moral support;
- creating a climate of trust;
- confronting problems and celebrating success;
- dealing with complex and unanticipated problems;
- becoming empowered and assertive;
- incorporating lateral accountability.

(Rose and Coles 2002)

Booth and Ainscow (2002) in the *Index for Inclusion* raise two questions in relation to special and mainstream school collaboration:

- Are students from the locality, currently in special schools, actively encouraged to attend the mainstream school?
- Are local special school staff invited to share their expertise with mainstream staff?

The process of inclusion shapes mainstream and special school collaborative partnerships because it focuses on removing barriers to learning and participation, tackling discrimination, and improving the effectiveness of educational and social outcomes for children with SEN and disability.

The Primary strategy recognises the value of such collaborative partnerships: 'many primary special schools already provide outreach to mainstream schools, for example, through sharing of expertise on working with children with a particular special educational need, or with behaviour management' (DfES 2003c: 6.61).

Box 1.3	Features of good inclusive practice

- A shared vision and commitment to inclusion.

- A stable and experienced teaching team working in collaboration with teaching assistants.

- Strong support from parents, carers and governors.

- Careful and systematic use of resources.

- Thorough monitoring, evaluation and assessment of progress.

- A calm and consistent school climate that promotes good, positive social relationships.

- High expectations of all pupils.

- Pupils' views are valued, and the pupils' voices are listened to.

- Clear and consistent whole-school policies, with the emphasis on early intervention.

- Recognition and respect for diversity.

- Appropriate, effective communication systems.

- Regular inter-school collaboration.

- The school is a community resource for learning and leisure activities.

Preparing for a changing role

Action planning

The inclusion action plan must be a convenient working document for teachers engaged in partnership inclusion activities. The inclusion action plan describes and summarises what needs to be done to implement and evaluate key inclusion priorities between mainstream and special schools.

The inclusion action plan must show:

- targets to be achieved in implementing particular inclusion goals;
- resources allocated to SEN and inclusion activities;
- the key individuals responsible for inclusion programmes;
- the completion dates for inclusion priorities and activities;
- the success criteria for SEN and inclusion activities.

The more effectively all inclusion team members can be involved in drawing up the action plan, the more likely it is to succeed. A good inclusion action plan for SEN will summarise the focus for development, and then set out the series of events and activities which will result in improvement. The plan should be made public within both partnership school settings, and therefore needs to be concise and accurate, in order to be understood by wide audiences.

The INCO in the mainstream school and the inclusion manager in the special school should be responsible for checking progress on the inclusion action plan. The leadership team in both inclusion partnership schools should receive regular up-dates and feedback on progress.

It is important that the SEN and inclusion action plan is reviewed in response to changing circumstances and the inclusion development work achieved within the mainstream setting.

Action plans for the inclusion of pupils with more complex SEN in mainstream schools should be negotiated with colleagues on the outreach inclusion team, in order to ensure maximum commitment and support from all participants.

An example of a joint SEN inclusion action plan can be found in Table 2.1, which supports the changing role of the special school and enhances mainstream school capacity building for inclusion.

Marketing

Special schools are in an extremely strong marketing position, when offering outreach support, training and consultancy on inclusion, to mainstream schools, as Rayner (1994) comments:

> The special school, and the support service, should aim to create a new interest in partnerships between schools which may provide support for SEN in a far more successful way than was previously realised. Ideally this relationship is based on mutual benefit, which involves a business-like organisation of provision, serving a clearly defined educational community. (Tilstone *et al.* 1998: 173)

Table 2.1 Joint mainstream and special school inclusion action plan

Action	Responsibility	Time scale	Resources	Success criteria
1. Joint whole school INSET on implcations of dual registration; meeting needs of ASD pupils; access and entitlement issues.	Special school inclusion manager and head teacher. (Parents and ASD pupils contributing to INSET day.) Mainstream INCO and head teacher.	2 June 2003.	Individual training CDs for all staff. Reproduction of handouts. Lunch and refreshments. One-day supply cover jointly funded to cover planning and preparation for INSET day.	All mainstream staff clear about needs of ASD pupils, and what dual registration entails. Positive staff attitudes about including more complex pupils.
2. Visit by mainstream staff to special school to see ASD pupils working, explore curriculum resources and link up with special school coach/mentor.	Inclusion manager and INCO, jointly.	4 July 2003.	Transport costs – use of school minibus. Supply cover costs for 12 mainstream teachers and one LSA (free), for one day out of school.	Mainstream staff fully aware of the P/NC levels pupils are functioning at. Mainstream staff establish regular contact with their special school coach/mentor (either electronic or face-to-face), and differentiate curriculum resources, in partnership.
3. Dual registered pupils have a taster day in mainstream, with their LSA. Mainstream Form 7S have a PSHCE lesson in tutor time, focused on how to support an ASD pupil, and using a Circle of Friends strategy.	Inclusion manager and LSA from special school, with INCO and head of forthcoming Year 8, in mainstream school.	10 July 2003.	One-day supply cover for INCO and inclusion manager, jointly funded.	ASD pupils experience an enjoyable visit. Mainstream staff and current Year 7 pupils are receptive, welcoming and supportive. Circle of Friends approach understood by mainstream pupils and their form tutor.
4. Joint parent/carers' network established for those with dual registered children, and electronic conferencing links.	Special school inclusion manager and Year 8 class teacher, with mainstream INCO and 8S form tutor.	Regular meetings set up at both schools (2.30pm–3.30pm, starting on 16 September 2003, and ongoing according to parents' needs.	Refreshment costs. Cost of parents' room refurbishment at mainstream school.	Improved communication and links with parents of ASD pupils. High level of parental satisfaction with provision in both schools. Reduction in parental concerns/ anxieties. Mainstream school recognised for its quality inclusion provision and oversubscribed. Both schools awarded quality mark for inclusion.
5. Joint Events Day to celebrate and recognise achievements of ASD dual-registered pupils, and others.	Special school inclusion manager and INCO with head of Year 8 from mainstream school	Event planning started in March 2004. Inclusion Event Day to take place on 10 July 2004.	Joint funding to cover costs of display materials, multi-media presentation, refreshments, advertising leaflets, and two days supply cover, for staff involved.	Event well attended by parents, LEA officers, and community members from both schools. Positive media coverage. Postive comments in visitors' book.

According to the Chartered Institute of Marketing (CIM) and Davies and Ellison (1996) marketing is a team effort and a management process whereby a school actively communicates and promotes its purpose, values, products and services to the pupils, parents, staff and the wider community. Marketing presents immense challenges for the special school sector. SEN and inclusion strengths need to be identified and exploited, in order to capitalise on meeting the inclusion needs of mainstream schools. The strengths that special schools have to offer their mainstream partners include:

- flexibility – being able to work in a range of mainstream contexts, covering a diversity of different needs;
- knowledge of local needs – identifying and filling the gaps that exist in SEN provision locally, and brokering special school outreach inclusion services to mainstream settings;
- credibility as specialists in SEN and inclusion – beacon or specialist school status, or an extended school;
- entrepreneurial experience – lending resources, running cost-effective INSET courses, workshops and seminars, producing and selling curriculum resource packs, inclusion training and guidance packs. Providing high quality materials such as: inclusion training and promotional videos, computer mouse mats and software, pens, and parent information guides to mainstream partners;
- the ability to repsond to the needs of mainstream settings, parents and the LEA;
- being innovative – staff are able to think 'outside the box', in promoting inclusion, e.g. offering visits to the 'virtual' inclusive classroom, or taster sessions in the cyber multi-sensory learning zone, putting on an inclusion exhibition in partnership with mainstream schools, and using video conferencing for dissemination of best practice.

It is vital that the special school, operating as an inclusion service within a federation or cluster of schools, surveys client satisfaction, as well as identifies current and future needs. An example of a client satisfaction survey can be found in Appendix 3.

Throughout the year of service, the special school would be well advised to advertise and promote its specialist services to new and prospective mainstream clients. This may include specific product launches, e.g. special offers on inclusion guidance booklets – 'Buy one, and get a second free', or, 'Ten per cent off first purchase'. An example of a promotional brochure for marketing a special school inclusion service is shown in Appendix 1.

Marketing tips

- Identify marketing opportunities. (The LEA may have a marketing 'expert', or consider contacting members of the local business community.)
- Produce a marketing plan which defines objectives, targets and performance measures/success criteria, linked to expenditure.
- Develop a coherent marketing strategy in order to manage change.
- Conduct ongoing market research.
- Actively market outreach and consultancy services and products on the special school website, or via a high quality 'glossy' folder, containing attractive information sheets.

- Improve the special school image and profile in the local learning community, by focused advertising.
- Forecast inclusion demands, set targets and sell services to the private and public sector.
- Consider employing a marketing consultant.
- Seek external sponsorship from local businesses, professional and specialist associations, or government funding.
- Secure a quality mark for inclusion services and products.

A marketing plan resembles a route map, which outlines how the special school intends to move from a specialist setting to become an outreach inclusion service and resource base.

A model marketing plan for a special school inclusion service is illustrated in Table 2.2 (see p. 20).

Table 2.2 Marketing plan for a special school inclusion service

Marketing fundamentals	Marketing priorities	Lead person	Actvities over next six months	Activities over 6–18 months
Products and services	Produce curriculum access packs. Plan training on inclusion for mainstream. Develop the outreach inclusion and consultancy team. Train mentors and assessors for quality assurance of IQM in mainstream schools.	Deputy head and inclusion manager.	Produce a range of curriculum packs for loan or sale. Roll out training programme to mainstream clusters.	Market curriculum resource packs. Become recognised training centre for SEN and inclusion training. Support the assessment and moderation of IQM in mainstream schools.
Price of services and products	Establish baseline for agreed SLA (with LEA and mainstream schools).	Head teacher of special school.	SLA agreed and distributed via LEA, to cluster mainstream partners.	SLA evaluated and offered to wider network of mainstream schools.
Promotion	Plan advertising and promotional literature for inclusion services and products.	Deputy head of special school and inclusion manager.	Promotional flyers and information packs produced and distributed to mainstream schools.	Website features inclusion service. Open day held. Inclusion exhibition and mini-conference in autumn term.
Place	Develop special school as an inclusive learning and resource centre.	Head teacher and inclusion manager in the special school.	Extend outreach support for more pupils and develop resource loan or purchase facility. Enable more complex mainstream pupils to receive specialist support in a special school setting, when appropriate.	Special school becomes a regular training venue for mainstream teachers, LSA/TAs, pupils, parents/carers. Assessment is provided by the special school. Parent/carer workshops and information centre established. Special school becomes part of the Inclusion Zone Federation of schools, within the LEA.
People	Plan programme of training to equip outreach team staff to support mainstream staff.	Deputy head and inclusion manager from special school.	Enable inclusion outreach team to deliver customised INSET, consultancy and support to mainstream schools.	Inclusion outreach services evaluated and improved. Inclusion team capacity reviewed and enhanced.
Process	Overview of client satisfaction. Evaluation and review of inclusion team's perspectives on inclusion partnerships with mainstream schools.	Deputy head in special school.	Questionnaire and surveys issued to mainstream staff, parents/carers, SEN pupils, and LEA. Evidence from discussions with inclusion team staff, on the effectiveness of services provided.	Findings from evaluation and market research lead to improvements being made.
Tangible evidence	Action research and case study evidence of best practice.	Deputy head and inclusion manager in special school.	Best practice inclusion case studies written up. Network and cluster meetings share best practice.	Action research and best practice case studies posted on inclusion website. Inclusion e-mail Forum and chat room established. Participation in LEA annual Inclusion Conference, where SEN pupils' experiences of inclusion are shared and celebrated.

SLA = Service Level Agreement

Developing staff inclusion roles

Special schools will play an increasing role in the provision of training for a range of client groups: mainstream teachers, student teachers, newly qualified teachers and learning support/teaching assistants, parents and carers. This will necessitate training for the providers themselves, however, to equip them for the new role.

Rouse and Florian (1996) in Campbell (2002) proposed that any staff development to support inclusion '. . . needs to address issues of collaboration, team building, problem-solving, evaluation, assessment and curriculum . . .'

Springfield *et al.* (1996) in Campbell (2002) indicated how special school staff could support mainstream teachers:

> . . . teachers cannot operate effectively to change classroom behaviours without concrete supports to guide their efforts, and time to learn and assimilate new behaviours . . . Strong assistance toward change, concrete models, coaching, and time produced change and, therefore, more commitment.

The DfES CPD initiatives such as Best Practice Research Scholarships, bursaries and sabbaticals are available to special school teachers who wish to focus on SEN and inclusion. The Fast Track teaching programme also encourages potential leaders to undertake placements within the special school sector. In addition, the NCSL is also including a module for potential and current head teachers, particularly those working in the mainstream sector, on how to lead and manage inclusion and pupils with SEN.

Advanced Skills Teachers (ASTs) in special schools continue to undertake valuable partnership outreach work with mainstream schools, which includes demonstrating and advising on best inclusive practice for pupils with SEN.

Leading literacy and numeracy teachers in special schools also demonstrate their excellent practice in enabling SEN pupils to access the literacy and numeracy strategies to mainstream colleagues. This training role also complements the work of the LEA's literacy and numeracy consultants, as well as that of the LEA SEN support service teachers.

It is crucial that identifying and meeting the needs of a diversity of children with AEN forms a key element of any Initial Teacher Training (ITT) or Newly Qualified Teacher (NQT) training programme, within the induction year. This could be delivered in the form of partnership training between a cluster of mainstream and special schools, especially where the special setting is a designated training school and a recognised training provider by an HE institution, for inclusion and SEN.

There needs to be more teacher, LSA/TA exchange between special and mainstream schools taking place. Where mainstream teachers and support assistants have worked in special schools for a specific period of time, they have been found to acquire a far greater range of SEN skills, which they have taken back, used and disseminated to other colleagues in the mainstream schools. This training approach may also contribute to improving the recruitment and retention of teachers working in the special school sector.

Special schools as training providers to mainstream schools can:

■ advise on teaching styles and access strategies for children and young people with SEN and disability;
■ advise on assessment, learning objectives and programme planning;

- model specialist teaching approaches and the use of specialist resources;
- advise on provision of differentiated teaching methods and resources;
- advise on adapting the curriculum;
- support the moderation of P scale assessments undertaken in mainstream schools;
- provide training for LSAs and TAs;
- provide training in behaviour management at varying levels;
- advise on the deployment and management of LSAs/TAs in the classroom.

The Index for Inclusion and the Inclusion Quality Mark (IQM) support special schools in their prime responsibility to enhance professional development in SEN and inclusion across the mainstream education network. They both emphasise the importance of role clarification and professional development in any joint collaborative inclusion partnership between special and mainstream schools.

Consultancy and outreach role

The TTA National SEN Specialist Standards (1999) were designed as an audit tool to help mainstream, special school and PRU teachers and head teachers, as well as teachers and managers in support services, to identify specific training and development needs in relation to the effective teaching of pupils with more severe and complex SEN, in a range of settings.

In particular, they set out an inter-related pattern of core, extension and role-based expertise, which helps to guide the development of appropriate SEN and inclusion training programmes.

Teachers and managers in special schools undertaking outreach work, and teachers and managers in support services, will need to focus on the Standards in relation to advisory, curricular and managerial roles and responsibilities. These key standards are illustrated in the form of an audit (Figure 2.1) at the end of this chapter. These specialist SEN standards will:

> . . . help them to identify knowledge, understanding and skills which they will need in helping schools to work towards increasing the inclusion of pupils with SEN in mainstream settings, widening their access to the curriculum, assisting teachers to differentiate teaching and learning more effectively, or supporting schools and parents/carers in establishing strong links between school and home-based learning. (TTA 1999: 1.3)

TTA also comment later in the SEN standards: 'Partnership arrangements will require some teachers with specialist knowledge of SEN to develop skills so that they can work effectively when advising and supporting other teachers or LSAs' (TTA 1999: 3.9).

In response to a growth in inclusive practice, special school staff will often assume a number of different roles. Mrs Smith may be a senior teacher, who is also a class teacher with curriculum leadership responsibilities; she may also provide advice and support for parents and carers and work in an outreach support capacity with mainstream schools. It is important that teachers with this sort of extended role are allowed adequate time to effectively fulfil their various duties.

The HMI (1995) in an unpublished report, identified 11 key areas of special school teacher expertise, linked to effectiveness:

1. Subject knowledge and expertise.
2. Skills in managing the disability.
3. Skills in lesson planning and preparation.
4. The effective organisation of teaching.
5. Skills in using questions to promote language.
6. Skills in giving feedback and praise to pupils.
7. Skills in enabling pupils to make choices and work independently.
8. Realistically high expectations of pupils.
9. The skilled assessment of pupils' achievements.
10. The ability to coordinate the contribution of other adults.
11. The ability to set the right climate for learning.

These areas of expertise relate to effective, inclusive classroom practice and curriculum access.

Although the TTA National SEN Specialist Standards provide a training framework guide, they do not outline the more strategic management skills that special school staff (teachers and LSAs) will require when supporting mainstream school colleagues in an outreach capacity.

The key skills required include:

- coaching and mentoring;
- team building;
- problem-solving and analysis;
- effective communication – both at an interpersonal level, and at a presentational level, i.e. delivering quality INSET or producing high quality modified curriculum materials;
- stress management.

The DfES, in their Report of the Special Schools Working Group, noted:

> Special schools can be involved in developing training materials to support the development of consultancy skills for special school staff undertaking, or planning to become involved in, outreach activities with mainstream schools. (DfES 2003b: 68)

Coaching

Coaches identified for their excellent practice, from special school leaders, teachers or LSAs/TAs, perform a similar role to that of ASTs or leading teachers. Coaching is concerned with unlocking an individual's potential to maximize his or her own performance.

Coaches offer others, i.e. senior managers, teachers or support staff in mainstream settings, effective, ongoing high quality professional development within school, which is focused on improving the quality of inclusive leadership, teaching and support, which in turn impacts on improving the quality of pupils' learning.

Special school coaches undertake their work collegially with mainstream colleagues in order to integrate and embed leaders', teachers' and support staff's professional learning with actual practice. They also provide ongoing constructive feedback, acting as a critical friend, and engage in reflective discussions about teaching, learning and leadership with their mainstream counterparts. They also help to build confidence, offer practical suggestions, and encourage, inspire and motivate others.

Coaches provide guidance and support in the form of:

■ modelling effective leadership, management, teaching and support strategies;
■ focusing on developing collaborative engagement, particularly in evaluating pupils work; and
■ directing staff to the most recent research or resources on best practice.

Special school or support service coaches, working in an outreach role with mainstream colleagues, require particular personal qualities and skills. These are as follows: a calm disposition, trust-building skills, mediation skills, listening skills, perseverance and patience, initiative and innovation skills, reflection skills, confidence, modesty and a non-patronising manner, credibility as practitioners, managers and/or leaders. They also need to know when to 'push' others, and when to 'back off', or sensitively withdraw.

The General Teaching Council (GTC) in the Teachers' Professional Learning Framework (TPLF) (2003) states that teachers need the opportunity to 'develop mentoring and coaching skills and their ability to offer professional dialogue and feedback' (GTC 2003: 6).

Team building

A special school outreach team is likely to be organised in such a way that all members work together for the common purpose of ensuring the smooth transition and inclusion of SEN pupils in a mainstream setting.

Team work as a cooperative process empowers others to adopt new and different opportunities. The characteristics of successful teams that promote inclusion in mainstream contexts are as follows:

■ clarity of role;
■ agreed shared values, purpose and procedures relating to inclusion;
■ clearly defined links with other teams, e.g. Key Stage teams;
■ sharing best practice, knowledge and information with others;
■ collective work approach to achieving shared goals;
■ collaborative working to explore differences, create consensus, solve problems and make decisions;
■ working relationships built on trust;
■ active listening;
■ monitoring and evaluating the effectiveness of inclusion programmes.

Belbin (1996) (in Fidler 2002) described key roles for team members:

■ Translating ideas about inclusion into practice (Implementer).
■ Utilising resources and driven by goals (Co-ordinator).

- Inspiring others and pushing them to make inclusion happen (Shaper).
- Advancing new ideas and synthesising knowledge (Innovator).
- Questioning, exploring and identifing external ideas and resources (Resource Investigator).
- Reviewing the work of the team, being an analytical and critical thinker (Monitor Evaluator).
- Being perceptive to other team members feelings, needs, concerns and being loyal to the team, favouring harmony (Team Worker).
- Being keen to complete inclusion tasks on time and according to plan (Completer Finisher).
- Having pre-existing specialist SEN and inclusion skills and knowledge (Specialist). (Fidler 2002: 55)

It will be the inclusion manager's role to work with and lead the special school outreach team, and to develop the focus and strategies that will enable all inclusion team members to realise their potential.

Problem-solving

The special school outreach inclusion team needs to be adept at problem-solving, in relation to supporting mainstream inclusion. There are several models of problem-solving which can be adopted by special school staff working with mainstream colleagues. The most appropriate model of solving problems for an inclusion team is Jackson's (1975) (in Fidler 2002), which views the process in five stages:

1. Identification, detection and definition of the problem (Formulation).
2. Developing an understanding of the SEN and inclusion problem or issue, and its implications (Interpretation).
3. Formulating a possible range of solutions to the problem (Constructing an alternative course of action).
4. Evaluating the possible solutions and selecting the most appropriate one (Decision-making).
5. Thorough planning, implementation and evaluation of the proposed SEN and inclusion change (Implementation). (Fidler 2002: 64)

Communication

Communication is the exchange of information in verbal or non-verbal forms. Hewitt (1996, in Blandford 1997) identified important communication competences which are relevant to the work of any special school staff engaged in mainstream inclusion programmes:

- *Administrative competences* – the ability to analyse information and data to identify important SEN and inclusion issues or elements; reach logical conclusions and make rational decisions based on sound evidence; be decisive, and plan and delegate appropriately.
- *Interpersonal competences* – the ability to motivate and inspire others to engage in SEN and inclusion activities and accept ownership; perceptive and intuitive to the needs of others, adapt accordingly and value others' opinions.

- *Communicative competences* – the ability to use appropriate body language and dress appropriately, in order to create the right image; the ability to make clear oral presentations and present information succinctly; the ability to express ideas clearly in writing; to write for different audiences and purposes.

The National Policy Board for Educational Administration (NPBEA) (1993), suggests helpful tips for producing effective presentations:

- Has clear title, identifying the content and meaning of the text.
- Uses appropriate headings and sub-headings.
- Visual impact created – no overcrowding on the page/slide.
- Utilises double-line spacing.
- Uses clear, legible font.
- Numbers titles, paragraphs, pages when necessary, for ease of reference.
- Summarises key points by using lists.
- Uses labelling on diagrams.
- Utilises capital letters, bold font, underlining and italics to emphasise important points.
- Adopts a consistent 'house style' for reports or presentations.

(Blandford 1997: 62)

Stress management

Stress management is a vital skill, essential to any special school outreach team. Stress may arise as a result of any of the following reasons:

- Unpredictability of SEN pupils or mainstream staff reactions to inclusion.
- Insufficient meeting time with colleagues, in and between schools.
- Parental dissatisfaction and complaints about aspects of inclusion.
- Paperwork overload.
- Resources or funding less than initially expected.
- Pace of change too fast.
- Negative attitudes or conflict of interests, causing 'blocks' to inclusion.

The senior management team, and in particular the inclusion manager from the special school, must promote stress management for any staff working in an outreach capacity. Although the common collaborative goal will be to include more complex SEN pupils with the minimum of disruption and as smoothly as possible, there will inevitably be the occasional unexpected outburst from pupils or staff.

Helpful strategies to reduce stress, as recommended by Brown and Ralph (1995) are as follows:

- The establishment of realistic and achievable inclusion goals.
- Allowing time for reflection.
- Providing a self-help group or support network for inclusion staff, where problems can be shared and solved together.
- Prioritising inclusion tasks and reviewing workloads.
- Increased delegation for inclusion responsibilities among team members.

- Providing CPD on conflict management, assertive training, positive thinking for inclusion team staff.
- Providing an 'in-house' staff counselling service.
- Promoting a culture or ethos that reassures staff that it is OK to show stress.
- Encouraging relaxation techniques for staff, i.e. aromatherapy, music therapy sessions, yoga, meditation, physical exercise.   (Blandford 1997: 36)

In addition to special school staff, in their consultancy role, imparting their specialist SEN and inclusion knowledge, advice and guidance to mainstream colleagues, they will also provide:

- an external perspective;
- examples of good inclusion experiences, encountered in other similar mainstream inclusion projects;
- a sounding board for mainstream colleagues and parents/carers to utilise;
- evaluative evidence.

In conclusion, special schools may find it beneficial to work within a network of other schools (mainstream and/or special school clusters) in order to facilitate their staff's entitlement to continual professional development.

The GTC, in their Teachers' Professional Learning Framework, comment:

Investing in professional development is the key to ensuring that schools become whole learning communities where teachers work together, learn from each other and share best practice on effective teaching and learning. . . . It is only through the collective work of teachers, and by creating a shared professional knowledge, that sustained school improvement and raised standards will be secured. (GTC 2003: 3)

In Figure 2.1 (page 28) the Standards in relation to SEN/inclusion roles are outlined. On page 30, there is a role specification for a special school head teacher as inclusion facilitator.

Figure 2.1 Standards in relation to key SEN/inclusion specialist roles

(These standards are appropriate for: outreach service SEN specialist teachers, SEN teachers/SENCOs in mainstream schools, and senior teachers/INCOs from special schools)

Indicate how confident you are about the aspects of each dimension by rating your skill level on a scale of 1 to 3 (1 = not yet acquired; 2 = developing ; 3 = securely in place)

1. Advisory roles and responsibilities

- Analyse others' teaching of pupils with more complex SEN, understand how improvements can be made and provide sensitive feedback, support, coaching and training to help others become more effective in their teaching _____

- Advise on assessing baseline performance using standardised tests and other measures, identifying strengths as well as needs, so that any progress resulting from special provision can be determined _____

- Advise on the effectiveness of, and when necessary justify the use of, specialised techniques and materials _____

- Advise on the work being undertaken by other teachers, LSAs, therapists and other support staff to ensure the integration of their specialist contributions _____

- Demonstrate effective ways of working with parents/carers and other professionals to ensure maximum curricular access, challenge and progression for SEN pupils _____

- Provide professional direction, including demonstration and/or specific training, so that others may understand or use specialised assessment, communication, ICT and mobility systems _____

- Cope effectively with frustration or conflict situations arising from the management of pupils with SEN, and work with colleagues and pupils in securing an environment which supports purposeful learning _____

- Lead training sessions for teachers, LSAs, parents/carers and others _____

2. Curricular roles and responsibilities

- Ensure that priorities outlined in the school improvement plan can be translated into policies and strategies which will ensure that pupils with more complex SEN have access to a relevant curriculum, including the National Curriculum _____

- Collaborate with pupils' teachers, subject leaders and/or key stage coordinators and other external specialists, to agree on specialised teaching programmes which reflect the prescribed IEP targets and arrangements for monitoring progress against those targets _____

- Advise on the development of lesson planning, ensuring that the priorities which are agreed for individual pupils are identified, and the strategies which aim to differentiate teaching and learning are appropriate _____

- Oversee the contributions of support staff to the delivery of the teaching programmes, to ensure that pupils' IEP targets are known, understood and achievable _____

- Monitor the use and effectiveness of specialised teaching resources, ensuring that they contribute to the achievement of intended outcomes _____

- Evaluate the extent to which curriculum planning and teaching result in discernible progress for all pupils _____

Figure 2.1 continued

3. Managerial roles and responsibilities

■ Understand what constitutes high quality SEN support strategies and create a team structure to achieve these ends

_____

■ Know the capabilities of staff engaged in SEN support work and deploy them effectively according to their strengths, ensuring staff receive clear feedback on the effectiveness of their contribution

_____

■ Monitor the deployment of staff to ensure that statutory functions, and functions requested by the LEA, schools and other agencies, are prioritised and met

_____

■ Audit, manage and monitor staff expertise to identify development and training needs, setting clear performance targets, agreeing action and identifying success criteria in respect of the targets

_____

■ Manage staff working in other schools/units, and negotiate with each school the specific blend of support activities required to meet the needs of the pupil

_____

■ Deploy staff in a balanced manner across individualised work, in-class support, resource development and adaptation, tutorial support and consultation, so that overall support is in line with the school or service's SEN/Inclusion policy and the learning priorities outlined for individual pupils

_____

■ Monitor and evaluate the contributions made by school or external support service staff to inter-agency team work

_____

■ Evaluate the use staff make of any delegated specialised equipment or delegated SEN resources

_____

■ Use evidence from the pupil, parent/carer, teacher and school to evaluate the system of support in operation and its impact on learning

_____

■ Check and readjust the work of staff in accordance with the changing needs of pupils, the changing level of staff expertise with SEN, and any requirements arising from local or national directives and strategies

_____

(Adapted from the TTA National SEN Specialist Standards 1999: 27–30)

Figure 2.2 Special school head teacher as inclusion facilitator

Role specification

Responsible to: Inclusion Strategy Manager

Responsible for: Developing inclusion partnerships between special and mainstream schools

Principal purpose: To promote and develop the role of special schools in facilitating and supporting mainstream schools inclusive policy and practice

Contract period: One-day secondment per week, for one year

Main duties

- Identify inclusive practices in the LEA's special schools
- Participate in the LEA Inclusion Work Group
- Inform future LEA planning in relation to developing the future role of special schools
- To attend any national and regional conferences and task groups related to inclusion and the future role of the special school
- To network with other LEA special school headteachers, where good inclusive practice exists between special and mainstream schools
- Support special school headteachers in identifying mainstream partners and assist in formulating inclusion action plans
- Participate in mainstream headteachers conferences, meetings and networks in the LEA
- Disseminate special school good inclusive practice to mainstream schools, clusters and services in the borough, via the intranet, newsletter and brochure
- Organise and coordinate an annual showcase event which publicises the outcomes of special and mainstream school inclusion activities, initiatives
- Provide advice, guidance and support to senior managers in special and mainstream schools, and support services, where appropriate on establishing inclusive partnerships
- Monitor the impact of inclusion activities across the special school spectrum, and produce an evaluation report.

Enhancing mainstream school capacity to become more inclusive

Key partnership factors

There needs to be clear identification of mutually agreed inclusion goals for any link programme or partnership activity, between the special and mainstream schools concerned. The appropriate selection of special school pupils who will benefit the most, academically and socially, from a mainstream inclusion experience, who will also act as ambassadors for future joint initiatives, is important.

Having a lead manager within the special school who acts as an identified point of contact for mainstream school INCO/SENCO is vital, to ensure that clear lines of communication exist between schools. This will help to support forward preparation and planning, especially in relation to coordinating day-to-day practices in timetabling, transport, health and safety issues, curriculum development and other organisational aspects.

Clear allocation of shared responsibilities and accountability for included SEN pupil outcomes is vital, i.e. who does what, by when, and how, particularly in relation to dual-registered pupils.

There must be an agreed commitment on behalf of special and mainstream schools in relation to issues connected to resource allocation, i.e. time, funding, staff deployment and training. A high level of collaboration, resource and expertise sharing is essential between partnership schools, based on mutual respect and recognition of what each school can contribute.

Rose and Coles (2002) identified the following pre-requisites for the successful inclusion of special school pupils in mainstream settings:

- appropriate staff training;
- sufficient levels of classroom support;
- raised awareness of mainstream staff about the complexity of SEN pupils' needs;
- promotion of positive attitudes among mainstream staff and pupils;
- positive whole-school ethos towards inclusion;
- readiness for inclusion;
- access improvements;
- a commitment to collaborative planning which involves all staff and pupils;
- regular special school support.

Fletcher-Campbell and Kington (2000), in their research into special and mainstream school inclusion partnership links, also identify:

- the location of schools;
- good transport facilities;
- suitable course, curriculum or projects;
- parental support;
- good planning and evaluation;
- LEA policy and support.

Rose and Coles (2002) indicate, in their research on special and mainstream collaboration for inclusion, that mainstream staff value most the following aspects of support, from a special school teacher:

- Meeting before placement to ensure clarity with regard to pupil's needs.
- Regular contact to discuss any inclusion problems, i.e. a telephone link or e-mail contact to a special school.

- Reassurance that mainstream staff are using appropriate strategies, and assisting pupil independence.
- Modelling approaches used by special school teachers, which are transferable within the mainstream classroom.
- Advice with regard to specific situations where knowledge and expertise are lacking.
- Information with regard to a specific disability.
- Provision of ideas for working with a more complex pupil.
- Advice on physical management and handling.
- Assistance with appropriate modes of communication.
- Advice with regard to the more effective use of specific resources or specialist equipment.
- Expectations made explicit about what pupils can do.

From a young person's perspective, mainstream schools can help to promote inclusion by:

- providing a special 'buddy' to help a child settle in to a new mainstream class;
- enabling special school children to have a 'voice' on the mainstream School Council;
- mainstream teacher talking to special school teacher to ensure included pupil gets the right type of help;
- having facilities for the administration of medication and care of unwell children;
- having positive IEPs which state what the SEN child can do;
- being aware of SEN pupil's needs, i.e. where to position in the classroom, how they learn best, knowing what special equipment is required;
- enabling mainstream LSAs to visit the child's special school and gain good ideas on how to assist the pupil on a dual placement;
- allowing SEN pupils to recruit their LSA, i.e. produce a video on a typical day in the life of the SEN pupil, which focuses on aspects of their learning and personal care or assistance needs, and giving this to the LSA to watch. This will give the LSA a very clear understanding of the child's individual needs, and level of independence;
- allowing children with more complex medical needs to have access to staff toilets or cloakrooms, where they can inject insulin in private or change a catheter, rather than using public pupil toilets;
- providing a 'safe haven' or quiet area where children with ADHD, BESD can unwind, receive counselling or appropriate therapy;
- class teachers and LSAs receiving training from health services regarding administering medication correctly, and how to deal with children who may have seizures, thus enhancing their access to out-of-hours learning activities and educational visits;
- offering more flexible timetabling to dual registered SEN pupils in order that they can attend appropriate courses and subject lessons, in both school settings;
- ensuring mainstream schools organise transport arrangements to allow special school children to participate in out-of-hours learning activities;
- involving pupils with SEN and disability in the writing of the school's Accessibility Plan, and consulting them fully in relation to access in education;
- providing outreach to families in relation to how to use a new access or communication aid.

Factors enhancing access

In relation to improving access in mainstream schools, Rose and Coles (2002) identify the following strategies as being useful:

- involving disabled pupils in identifying strategies that would improve access;
- taking a group or class of mainstream pupils to visit disabled pupils working in the special school setting, in order to raise their awareness and understanding of disability and access issues in the mainstream context;
- instigating a 'buddy' system where named pupils assist special school SEN and disabled pupils to travel around the mainstream school setting safely, and settle into their new class;
- implementing new school rules to ensure special school SEN pupil safety, and altering routes around the school;
- making necessary modification to mainstream classrooms.

What mainstream can offer special schools

Fletcher-Campbell and Kington (2000), in their research on links between special schools and mainstream schools, indicate what mainstream schools require from their special school counterparts.

> Mainstream schools want either a very high quality specialist 'state-of-the-art' input from special schools acting as resource centres, to fill the gaps in their own expertise and knowledge, or very basic 'hands on' practical help where staffing in the school is stretched to the limit.

Although mainstream schools see special schools as the providers of specialist expertise and resources, mainstream schools can offer special schools, in return, particular knowledge, skills and expertise related to the curriculum and subject leadership.

The mainstream school can offer the following to special school partners:

- Specialist curriculum facilities on a larger scale, i.e. science laboratories and equipment; a wider range of music equipment and recording studios, up-to-date design and technology equipment and facilities, which help to broaden curriculum coverage and access for special school pupils.
- Extensive subject expertise in curriculum areas, e.g. music, modern foreign language.
- More extensive knowledge and experience about delivering national strategies, such as the primary or Key Stage 3 strategies.
- Greater experience in team building and working in teams.
- More experience as middle managers, of subject leadership and subject co-ordination.
- A wider range of out-of-hours learning activities.
- Positive peer role models for special school pupils.
- Real-life experiences in a wider learning community environment, to help develop pupils' PSHCE skills.

- Modern 'high-tech' multi-media facilities on a larger scale, for the production of high quality 'glossy' promotional and informational literature, for a range of audiences.
- More experience of marketing their school and its strengths, within the wider community.
- Greater experience of exploring and developing community links, e.g. seeking sponsorship from local businesses.

Inhibitors to inclusion partnerships

Fletcher-Campbell and Kington (2000), identified the following 'blockers' to developing inclusion partnership links with mainstream schools.

- Lack of funding.
- Negative staff attitudes.
- A school's apathy and not wanting to link.
- Lack of time.
- Work or initiative overload.
- Competing academic pressures on mainstream schools.
- Staffing difficulties and insufficient support staff.
- Location of school in terms of geographical distance between schools.
- Administrative and organisational difficulties.
- Poor liaison or relationships between schools.
- Lack of appropriate staff training.
- Inflexible school timetables.
- Non-educational provision not being made available, i.e. no facilities for the administration of medication or personal care.

Receiving special school staff/pupils

In preparation for receiving special school staff and pupils within a mainstream school context, certain questions have to be answered, in relation to whether the inclusion experience will be worthwhile and positive for all those concerned. Fletcher-Campbell and Kington (2000) suggest the following questions:

- What is the nature and purpose of the links?
- Whose needs are being served?
- What needs are being served?
- Who was involved in the initial decision-making?
- What are the reference points for the exact structure of the links?
- What are the strategies for monitoring and review?
- What are the processes and criteria for evaluation?
- Are the links embedded in the relevant school development plans?
- How are the links being resourced?
- How are training needs, consequential on the link arrangements, being identified and met?
- How will the culture and curriculum structure of each school change as a result of the link arrangements?

The inclusion coordinator from the mainstream school, and the inclusion manager from the special school together, should pre-plan and prepare for the inclusion of the SEN pupil from the special school. The checklist (Figure 3.1) is a useful point of reference for the INCO and the inclusion manager.

> . . . Schools are children's natural communities. If a child with a disability or SEN is not fully included in the playground and after school activities, they will not have real friends. In effect, their education may be inclusive but they are still standing 'on the edge' and missing out on important areas of personal development. Being lonely is a special need in its own right. (DfES 2003b: 123)

Inclusion contracts

A contract is a formal written agreement, which is drawn up in negotiation with the special school and the receiving mainstream school, in order to secure the inclusion of dual placement pupils.

The contract outlines the inclusion expectations from both partnership schools, in respect of the agreed level of additional funding and resourcing. The head teachers from each school sign the contract, and the implications of providing appropriate provision, monitoring and evaluating the outcomes of the inclusion experience are made explicit.

In addition, the SEN pupil and his or her parents/carers can be provided with an Inclusive Learning Contract, which is a simplified version of the more formal school inclusion contract.

Examples of both types of inclusion contracts are illustrated in Figures 3.2 and 3.3.

Mainstream training

A lack of knowledge about special educational needs is a barrier to inclusion. Mainstream teachers may have 'fear of the unknown' and experience anxiety and fear about having to meet the learning difficulties of a more complex SEN child in a large mainstream class of mixed ability pupils. Training from special school teachers which raises their awareness, increases their understanding of more complex SEN, and gives them opportunities to develop practical skills to meet the needs of these pupils in the classroom, enhances mainstream teachers' confidence, and allays any fears.

Not every mainstream teacher is expected to be an expert in more complex SEN, but they do need to know the basic skills required of all teachers, which include curriculum differentiation, target setting for individual pupils and behavioural management. Mainstream teachers also need to know how to deploy LSAs/TAs effectively within their classroom, in order to ensure that their support impacts positively on pupils' learning. Any professional development for inclusion must focus on extending teaching repertoires, the mutual sharing of good practice, and reflection and action enquiry.

Learning support services and educational psychology services have a crucial role to play in advising teachers on effective strategies for responding to the diverse needs of pupils in mainstream classrooms, in order to embed school-wide inclusive practice.

Figure 3.1 Pre-inclusion checklist

☐ All mainstream staff teaching and supporting the pupil, know his/her current national curriculum and/or 'P' scale levels of attainment.

☐ All mainstream staff understand fully the nature of the pupil's special educational needs.

☐ All mainstream staff working with the pupil are aware of the child's strengths and areas requiring further development and improvement.

☐ Staff in the mainstream school are clear about the pupil's preferred learning style(s) and preferred method(s) of communication.

☐ Mainstream staff are clear about the role of any additional specialist teachers, LSAs, TAs supporting the pupil.

☐ Mainstream pupils in the class are prepared for the reception of the incoming pupil through discussion in PSHCE sessions.

☐ Mid-day supervisors and office staff in the mainstream school are prepared for the inclusion of the pupil.

☐ Specialist equipment or improvements to access have been secured prior to placement.

☐ A visual inclusion timetable has been prepared for the pupil, which indicates the stages of induction in the mainstream school.

☐ The special school pupil has been provided with mainstream school information, e.g. a colour coded plan of the school; a list of staff who will teach or support the pupil with accompanying photographs to aid identification; list of out-of-hours learning activities; routines and reward systems.

☐ The pupil has the opportunity to meet his or her study buddy, peer mentor, pupil befriender or peer counsellor, prior to joining the school.

☐ Any special transport arrangements are pre-planned, to take account of later pick-up times, following out-of-hours learning activities.

☐ The special school pupil and parents/carers have an opportunity to visit the mainstream school, as often as necessary, prior to mainstream placement.

☐ Parents/carers of the SEN pupil are kept fully informed during all preparatory stages for mainstream inclusion.

Figure 3.2 School contract for inclusion

This contract is a formal agreement which holds both partnership schools accountable for including dual registered SEN pupils in a mainstream and specialist setting, within the Sunny Town Learning Zone Campus, and for ensuring appropriate provision is put in place.

Leafy Lane School will provide:	**Waterfall Community School will ensure:**
In-class support in mainstream lessons	A high level of pastoral care for pupils
Advice on curriculum access	Peer 'buddying' operates
Guidance on inclusive teaching approaches for learning	Participation in out-of-hours learning
Advice on assessment, target setting and IEPs/ILPs	An appropriate curriculum entitlement
INSET on SEN, inclusion and disability access	Opportunities arise for pupils to express their views about inclusion, and provision
Advice and support to parents	Meeting time is planned for mainstream staff to liaise with Leafy Lane inclusion team members

The provision for, and progress of dual registered SEN pupils, will be monitored closely by both schools, each term, in addition to being evaluated and reviewed annually, in accordance with the SEN Code of Practice 2001, and the SEN and Disability Act 2001, and its related Code of Practice (Schools).

This contract is renewable, after twelve months, or before, if dual placement breaks down.
Signatures:

Headteacher (Leafy Lane School): _____ Date: _____

Headteacher (Waterfall Community School): _____ Date: _____

Figure 3.3 Inclusive learning contract

I, John Walker, agree to take full part in all activities that include me working alongside pupils at Waterfall Community School.

 I will meet with my key teacher every day, and talk about any worries I may have about inclusion, as well as my successes.

 I will join in as many out-of-hours learning activities as I can.

 I will consider other people's feelings, and behave sensibly at all times.

 I will work to the best of my ability, and ask if I don't know what to do.

 I will work hard to meet the targets set on my Inclusive Learning Plan

Signed:

Pupil: _____ Date: _____

Parent/Carer: _____ Date: _____

Figure 3.4 Inclusive learning plan

Name: _____ Form/class: _____ Plan start date: _____ Action ☐ Action + ☐ Statement ☐ In-class support ☐ *(tick boxes)*

Pupil profile: Jane has poor concentration and coordination skills; difficulty with written recording; experiences frustration and resulting temper-tantrums when presented with very dense text. She has a specific learning difficulty. Her strengths are in art and ICT. She enjoys using the computer and learns best visually. She is functioning at NC Level 2 in English, Level 3 in mathematics and science, at the beginning of Year 7.

Cross-curricular learning targets	Strategies to meet the targets set		Evidence of progress in meeting targets
In all lessons I will:	☐ Writing frames	☐ Modified worksheets	
1. Follow step-by-step instructions	☐ Computer access	☐ Interactive whiteboard	
	☐ Overhead projector	☐ Multi-media	
	☐ Visual prompts, e.g. tables, charts, graphs, diagrams, flow-charts, pictures, photographs	☐ One-to-one explanation	
2. Control my anger using 'tips to stay cool'		☐ Subject-specific vocabulary lists	
	☐ Mind-maps	☐ Brain gym	
	☐ Teacher modelling	☐ Group work	
3. Stay on task for ten minutes, without a break	☐ Working to music	☐ Peer 'study buddy' support	
	☐ Pair work		
	☐ Oral participation		**Next steps:** (What the pupil needs to do to improve or reach his or her next target)
	(Tick the strategies used to help pupil reach targets)		

Date of review: _____ Subject: _____ Teacher's signature: _____ Pupil's signature: _____

In a report on the use of temporary teachers, OFSTED noted that these staff were very rarely provided with information about pupils' attainment, or the nature of their special educational needs. It is therefore vital that inclusive schools engage supply teachers in continuing professional development (CPD), focused on SEN and inclusion, in order to develop their knowledge and teaching skills. All teaching and non-teaching staff should be clear about the principles, processes and outcomes of inclusive practice. By offering training to mainstream school head teachers on 'How Inclusive is Our School', OFSTED hope to address some of the issues outlined above.

The Audit Commission report on mainstream practice said:

The more inclusive the classroom, the greater the diversity of needs among its pupils – and, in turn, the greater the challenge teachers face to tailor lessons to suit the aptitudes of each and every pupil. Many teachers feel under considerable pressure, on the one hand to meet the needs of individual pupils, and on the other to deliver a demanding national curriculum and achieve ever-better test results; research suggests that many feel ill-equipped for this task. (Audit Commission 2002a: 95)

In the same Audit Commission report, mainstream school SENCOs were asked to identify the staff training priorities related to core classroom skills, that were essential to SEN and inclusion (Table 3.1).

Table 3.1 Staff training priorities related to core classroom skills

Aspect of staff training needs	Priority of need
Behaviour management	* * *
Target setting/writing and using IEPs	* * *
New SEN Code of Practice	* * *
Teaching Literacy	* *
Working with assistants/inclusive classrooms	* *
Dyslexia/specific learning difficulties	* *
Identifying needs/early identification	* *
General understanding of SEN	*
Speech and language difficulties	*
Working with other agencies	*

(Audit Commission 2002a: 37)

Audit tools like the Index for Inclusion or the Inclusion Quality Mark (IQM) help to support the CPD of mainstream staff, by identifying aspects of inclusive practice that require further improvement, especially in relation to curriculum delivery, teaching and learning.

The Teachers' Professional Learning Framework (TPLF) introduced by the General Teaching Council (GTC) in 2003, outlined the knowledge base and practice teachers required in relation to improving inclusive practice. This entailed teachers understanding:

- how learning occurs;
- cognition and intelligence;
- pedagogy;
- subject knowledge;
- teaching approaches and learning styles; and
- the social and cultural context in which these are applied.   (GTC 2003: 15)

The TPLF offers a map of professional development experiences which helps individual teachers to plan for professional learning:

> Learning runs right through a teaching career. It takes place every day, formally and informally, through a wide range of learning experiences, deepening and revitalising teachers' skills, abilities, values and knowledge. (GTC 2003: 2)

Appendix 6 shows an adapted version of the GTC TPLF, which will enable all teachers engaged in facilitating the inclusion of SEN pupils in a range of educational settings, to keep a record of their professional learning achievements.

Core SEN specialist standards

The core TTA National SEN Specialist Standards (1999) enable mainstream school head teachers to prepare for the increasing inclusion of more complex SEN pupils, by auditing existing SEN expertise within the school, and identifying the school's future specialist SEN training needs, especially where the school is working in partnership with a special school.

The TTA comment:

> As the Government's intention to increase opportunities for pupils with severe and/or complex SEN to be educated within mainstream schools is realised, teachers will need a basic understanding of the range of SEN to be found in most mainstream classes, and more teachers in mainstream schools will require knowledge, understanding and skills to work effectively with pupils with severe and/or complex SEN. (TTA 1999: 1.9)

The core SEN specialist standards cover five aspects:

1. Strategic direction and development of SEN provision nationally and regionally.
2. Identification, assessment and planning.
3. Effective teaching, ensuring maximum curriculum access.
4. Development of key skills in communication, literacy and numeracy, and ICT capability.
5. Promotion of social and emotional development, positive behaviour and preparation for adult life.

In relation to the strategic direction and development of SEN, all mainstream teachers will need a working knowledge and understanding of key SEN principles, definitions and basic inclusive practices. They will also need to recognise, value and raise the achievements of more complex SEN pupils within their

Figure 3.5 What to include in a mainstream school inclusion training programme

Whole school	**SMT/Governors/INCO/SENCO**
Definition, concept and principles of inclusion	Inclusion and school improvement
Entitlements of learners	Action planning for inclusion
Access issues – implementing the DDA and SENDA 2001	Access plans
Benefits of inclusion	Strategic management of inclusion
Features of effective inclusive schools	Effective deployment of resources
Dual registration	Monitoring and evaluating inclusion culture, policy and practice (value added)
Subject/Pastoral leaders	**Subject/Class teachers**
Subject action plans for inclusion	Practical classroom strategies to implement the NC inclusion statement of principles
Assessment for learning and SEN	
Tracking SEN pupil progress	Implementing ILPs, IEPs, PSPs
Using performance data to inform SoW, PoS for SEN pupils	Using assessment data to inform planning, teaching and learning for SEN pupils
Managing resources for inclusion	Deploying LSAs/TAs effectively
Monitoring and evaluating inclusion	Managing challenging pupil behaviour
LSAs/TAs	**Pupils**
Effective inclusive support strategies	Becoming an 'inclusion be-friender', 'study buddy', peer mentor/counsellor
Supporting the implementation of ILPs, IEPs	
Assessing impact of support on learning	Becoming an inclusive learner
Managing challenging pupil behaviour	Brain breaks
Supporting SEN pupils' personal care and health needs	How to manage stress and anger

Parents/Carers

Concept and benefits of inclusion and dual registration

How parents'/carers/ can support inclusive learning

(This inclusion training programme guide has been informed by the TTA National SEN Specialist Core Standards (1999), and the GTC Teachers' Professional Learning Framework (2003))

classes. In order to do this, they need to extend and deepen their basic knowledge and skills of identification, assessment and planning related to SEN.

Mainstream teachers also need to know how and when to use effective appropriate teaching strategies and lesson structures with SEN pupils. They need to offer these pupils opportunities for collaborative learning, and plan the content, delivery and pace of their lessons to take account of SEN pupils' individual learning needs. Mainstream teachers need to understand the reasons underlying more complex SEN pupils' behaviour that result in barriers to learning. Greater tolerance is required, especially when a child's behaviour is the result of the side-effects of medication, and not within the direct control of the child.

A modified version of the TTA core SEN specialist standards follows (Figure 3.6) which provides a CPD inclusion audit for mainstream teachers.

Managing dual placements

Any dual placement, whereby a special school pupil spends a proportion of his or her week, i.e. 51 per cent or more, in a mainstream setting, requires careful planning. Pre-preparation and clear guidance regarding the support required, in advance of the pupil commencing in the mainstream school, are crucial.

Mainstream staff need to understand the purpose of the dual placement, what the pupil's individual learning needs are, and the expectations related to pupil outcomes. The process can be made more manageable if the dual placement pupil's LSA/TA works with them, across both school settings, in order to ensure greater continuity in learning and inclusion, as well as promoting smoother transition.

The process of dual placement is also enhanced by mainstream staff who will work with the special school pupil, visiting that pupil, prior to placement, in his or her special school setting. This will enable mainstream colleagues to observe their subject being taught and also to view the range of curriculum resources available to enhance subject access.

QCA commented in their general guidance on planning, teaching and assessing the curriculum for pupils with learning difficulties:

> Curriculum development and planning for pupils with learning difficulties can be greatly improved when colleagues working in special and mainstream settings work together. Staff in both settings have particular skills, understanding and expertise which should be valued and shared. . . . The sharing of expertise allows schools to work together on the development of an inclusive curriculum that fully supports pupils with learning difficulties working in a range of settings. (QCA 2001: 11)

The senior management team in mainstream schools particularly, must pro-actively support their staff in relation to helping them to develop their confidence in including a wider diversity of SEN pupils in their classroom. Opportunities therefore must be provided for continuing professional development which includes: observing and modelling special school staff teaching and support approaches; modifying curriculum materials together; utilising appropriate assessment and moderation systems; and keeping an ongoing open dialogue between mainstream and special school colleagues.

Figure 3.6 Core SEN and inclusion specialist standards for mainstream teachers

Indicate how confident you are about the aspects of each dimension by rating your skill level on a scale of 1 to 3 (1 = not yet acquired; 2 = developing; 3 = securely in place).

A. Strategic direction and development of SEN provision

■ understand changing SEN perceptions in legislation and government documentation, e.g. SEN Code of Practice _____

■ knowledge and understanding of key SEN and inclusion terms and concepts _____

■ understand stereotyping and equal opportunities _____

■ know how special schools, support services and other specialist provision supports mainstream inclusion _____

■ understand partnership and cluster arrangements between special and mainstream schools, which facilitate inclusion _____

■ take account of parents/carers', voluntary and advocacy agencies expectations _____

■ understand roles and responsibilities of SEN specialist teachers _____

■ make use of relevant research and evidence to justify making changes to assessment, curriculum and teaching arrangements, e.g. inspection reports, school self-evaluation findings _____

■ understand disability rights and access issues _____

B. Identification, assessment and planning

■ take into account the strengths and limitations of different forms of assessment for more complex SEN pupils _____

■ make effective use of specialised informal and formal assessment, and use to inform planning, teaching and support _____

■ judge pupils' progress on meeting IEP targets, and engage pupils and parents/carers in the target setting process _____

■ judge the added value provided by teaching and learning, from evidence gathered on SEN pupil progress _____

■ know how to access examination concession arrangements for SEN pupils with more complex needs _____

■ prepare and write accurate assessment reports for SEN pupils' reviews _____

■ work jointly with external SEN agencies, services and special school staff to plan and implement programmes and compile reports _____

C. Effective teaching, ensuring maximum curriculum access

■ knowledge of appropriate curriculum and assessment criteria to inform curriculum delivery and access for SEN pupils _____

■ understand NC inclusion statement and QCA NC guidance related to more severe and complex SEN pupils with learning difficulties _____

■ analyse complex learning sequences and set smaller achievable targets for SEN pupils _____

■ identify individual learning outcomes and develop, implement and evaluate a range of approaches to help SEN pupils achieve outcomes _____

■ reduce barriers to learning _____

■ encourage SEN pupils to become more independent learners _____

■ adapt and modify teaching and pupil resource materials to match their preferred learning style and maturity level _____

■ use, manage and evaluate relevant specialised aids and resources, including ICT, that enhance curriculum access _____

■ take account of the effects on learning and behaviour of medications, medical treatments and therapies _____

■ work collaboratively with specialist and non-specialist staff to make effective use of teaching and learning environments _____

D. Development of communication, literacy and numeracy skills and ICT capability

■ understand the pupils' level of receptive and expressive language skills, and plan a structured programme of development

■ provide a wide range of actual and simulated opportunities for the development of receptive and expressive language

■ work collaboratively with others, e.g. LSAs, SALTs, specialist teachers, to extend pupils' listening, speaking, reading and writing skills

■ appreciate and allow for difficulties some pupils have in acquiring and using literacy and numeracy skills

■ know and apply the effective pedagogy relating to the teaching of literacy, numeracy, ICT and study skills, and relate these to the needs of pupils with complex and severe SEN

■ make effective use of real life experiences beyond the classroom, to help SEN pupils understand the importance of literacy, numeracy and ICT skills in everyday life

E. Promotion of social and emotional development, positive behaviour and preparation for adult life

■ work with parents/carers, social services and other agencies to agree approaches to each pupil's personal development, taking account of any cultural or ethnic factors

■ structure tasks and learning so SEN pupils can know what is expected of them, and persevere and concentrate

■ use reward systems and peer and adult mentoring to promote positive interpersonal relationships between pupils and adults

■ exploit and use the whole curriculum and general school life and work, to enhance pupils' emotional growth and life skills

■ promote pupils' PSHCE and sex and relationship education knowledge and skills, to help them meet challenges arising from a disability, personal behaviour, interpersonal relationships, leisure pursuits and family life

■ encourage pupils to persevere with their learning tasks when difficulties arise

■ take account of a range of learning styles which suit individual SEN pupils, in order to motivate them

■ develop positive, consistent and non-confrontational approaches to disruptive behaviour and implement an appropriate range of management techniques

■ link classroom teaching with any curricular and extra-curricular accreditation, e.g. Youth Award Scheme, Duke of Edinburgh Award Scheme

■ encourage the development of independent living skills and life skills, and prepare pupils for post-school training opportunities

(Adapted from TTA National SEN Specialist Standards 1999: 9–12)

Senior management within the special school, in relation to dual placements, need to support mainstream capacity building in the partnership school. This will entail the effective deployment of a focused outreach team comprising teachers and LSAs, deployed specifically to support dual placement pupils in mainstream settings. The staff, as well as the dual registered pupils, require a key contact person within the mainstream school, who may be a deputy head, INCO or SENCO. They need to be made to feel part of the mainstream context and culture. Mainstream colleagues need to be very clear about the special school staff inclusion facilitation role.

Dual placements have the advantage of embedding inclusion experiences within the culture, policy and practice of the mainstream school, making them clearly part of the school improvement process.

Fletcher-Campbell and Kington (2000) noted in their research that:

> While links are regarded as optional extras and not embedded into the plans of every special and every relevant mainstream school, there will continue to be a divide between the two forms of provision.

The embedding of good inclusive practice is very much dependent upon the outcomes, aspirations and funding arrangements being made explicit from the outset. There needs to be a greater financial incentive offered to mainstream schools in order to encourage them to offer more dual registration placements, thereby promoting greater inclusion. With forthcoming standards fund changes, it will be necessary, via the Schools Forum, to encourage clusters of mainstream schools with a special school, to pool funding, in order to sustain dual placements. The Financing of Maintained Schools Regulations provide that when a pupil is dual registered, both the special and the receiving mainstream school should each receive a level of funding equivalent to that of a full-time pupil placement.

Parents and carers need to be kept fully informed about dual placements, in relation to their purpose, principles of operation, and how they contribute to raising standards, and in particular, how they can benefit their own child. A focused parents' workshop or presentation in mainstream and special school settings can help to allay any anxieties that parents/carers may have. Special school staff may be best placed to work with parents in this way. It can also be useful to provide a parents'/carers' guide to dual placements (an example of this type of guide is provided in Appendix 5).

The DfES Report of the Special Schools Working Group featured the following parental comment regarding dual placements:

> I don't see any point in disrupting my child between two sites unless there is a real programme which benefits him socially and educationally. These arrangements need to be carefully planned so that everybody benefits. Otherwise it is just stressful and confusing for the child. (DfES 2003b: 135)

Obtaining the child's or young person's views about dual-placement experiences is also very important. They need to be able to communicate their thoughts and feelings to other prospective dual-placement pupils, and to indicate the positives as well as the pitfalls, which may arise from the inclusive experience. This in turn will help those staff working with these pupils in both settings to ensure that they fully understand the nature of the support and learning experiences that will fully meet their academic as well as their personal, social, health and emotional needs.

It is vital that any good practice existing in schools that relates to dual placements is disseminated and promoted at LEA as well as at school cluster level. External mechanisms, such as OFSTED, the Inclusion Quality Mark (IQM), or LEA school self-evaluation SEN and inclusion audits, can all ideally recognise, acknowledge and accredit or validate such good practice.

Dual registration must also be viewed as a two-way process, as it can operate in the reverse direction, i.e. more complex mainstream pupils may spend at least 50 per cent of their time per week in a special school setting, in a Pupil Referral Unit (PRU), or in a specialist unit attached to another local mainstream school.

Fletcher-Campbell and Kington (2000) in their research on links between special and mainstream schools noted:

> If the special school is perceived as part of the continuum of educational provision and a resource centre with its own particular expertise, then it is logical to expect complementary movement from mainstream schools to special schools.

Figure 3.7 Checklist for inclusive classroom practice

Year Group/class/set _____ **No. of additional adults** _____

Context: (pupil grouping, gender balance, number of children with SEN at each graduated response; subject/topic of lesson)

_____

_____

Inclusive teaching and learning strategies	Evidence/Comment
Appropriate range of resources, materials and concrete apparatus	
Pupils' seating is purposely planned throughout the lesson	
Classroom rules are displayed and referred to when necessary	
A clear link is made to previous learning	
The lesson objectives are shared with pupils	
Teacher makes instructions explicit and pupils understand these	
Teacher models and clearly explains new concepts, skills, knowledge	
Subject specific or new vocabulary is displayed and referred to in lesson	
Classroom displays are used effectively and interactively	
ICT/IT is used effectively in lesson (interactive whiteboard, computer, multi-media)	
There are opportunities for pupils to ask questions	
Differentiated questioning is utilised by the teacher	
Differentiated levels of tasks/activities are set which match ability range	
Timescales are made explicit by the teacher, for thinking, task completion	

Pupils are active learners, e.g. paired work, group work, 'buddying'	
Multi-sensory teaching approaches are utilised	
Scaffolding supports learning, i.e. writing frames, mind-mapping	
LSAs/TAs actively promote and assess SEN pupils' learning throughout the lesson	
There is a quiet work area in the classroom for pupils who need it	
There is opportunity for independent work, supported by visual prompts and resources	
Effective and positive behaviour management strategies are utilised throughout the lesson	
All pupils contributions in the lesson are valued	
Learning is reviewed and checked at the end of the lesson	
There are opportunities to feed back using a variety of media	
Misunderstandings and mistakes are dealt with sensitively, and utilised as teaching points	
Appropriate differentiated homework tasks are provided	

Observer: _____

Date: _____

(Adapted from the DfES 2002, NLNS: including all children in the literacy hour and daily mathematics lesson)

Quality first inclusion partnerships

Clusters

Clusters and networks help to promote inclusive practice in schools, through the pooling of expertise, synergy and collaborative working. Collaboration is a strategy which supports school improvement.

Clusters are where two or more schools collaborate and come together for mutual benefit, to help meet particular needs, such as SEN and inclusion. There is a commitment to share resources, decision-making and responsibilities. Regular meetings are held which focus on planning, sharing best practice, reviewing and monitoring progress towards inclusion.

Clusters of mainstream schools must involve a special school, in order to benefit from outreach support, advice and consultancy. Clusters can be a single phase or a multi-phase. They can include external agencies such as health, social services, voluntary organisations and local businesses within the learning community.

Purpose of clusters

Clusters allow a group of schools to:

- achieve economies of scale by pooling resources;
- develop specialisms, and the inter-change of skills throughout the cluster;
- facilitate closer links between mainstream and special schools, and cross-phase;
- assist LEA decision-making and inform SEN and inclusion strategy;
- provide a clearer focus to SEN and inclusion service delivery.

Clusters require a key person to co-ordinate them, which could be a head teacher, from one of the cluster schools. Participation in cluster activities is time-consuming for schools, and there needs to be consideration given to funding supply cover for teaching staff involved.

The development of a cluster tends to be sequential. The first stage is the initiation, where initial functional contact is made with an LEA SEN and inclusion officer. The second stage involves consolidation, where the cluster has an agreed focus, i.e. partnership development between special and mainstream schools, in order to promote inclusion of more complex SEN pupils. The final stage is re-orientation, where a corporate identity is established, as well as an agreed cluster policy, shared INSET, external expertise consultation and evaluation of inclusion cluster activities.

It is vital that LEAs engage special schools in mainstream cluster activities, in order to ensure that they are included in any inclusion training programmes and the dissemination of information.

Networks

Networks are mechanisms where participants collaborate for mutual benefit, and exchange skills and resources in order to solve problems. They also enable those from special and mainstream schools to share experiences, discuss issues of concern related to inclusion, reflect on their professional learning, improve inclusive practice, share action research findings and disseminate best practice.

Those networks focused on mainstream inclusion capacity building are seen to support teacher learning and professionalism, as well as motivate and empower those involved in partnership developments.

Networks can also be 'virtual networks', where professionals can support each other and share best practice via an on-line learning community. Networks also provide an excellent forum for special schools to market their skills to mainstream schools, and the LEA.

Networks bring together those with shared interests, commitment and expertise in SEN and inclusion. They:

- encourage teachers from special and mainstream schools to learn from each other;
- enable professionals to explore and challenge values and ideas relating to SEN and inclusion;
- provide a discussion forum for participants to exchange experiences on approaches and strategies that promote inclusive practice;
- provide information and coaching on specific skills for managing inclusion;
- contribute towards strengthening professional dialogue between special and mainstream schools.

The DfES report of the special schools working group notes that funding structures to support partnership working should 'Promote collaborative working between special and mainstream schools, through participating in twinning arrangements, federations and clusters' (DfES 2003b: 10 para. 12). The same report goes on to state that special schools could focus on developing support networks for parents, thereby promoting greater confidence in the movement of SEN pupils and staff, between sectors.

Networks and clusters should not be confused with federations, which are where two or more schools join together under the same management, having one shared head teacher, e.g. a co-located special and mainstream school on a single campus. Federations seek to build on existing collaboration and good practice in their schools, providing support for staff and school leaders to help raise standards in teaching and learning across all the schools.

Inclusive learning communities

A learning community involves school staff, parents, pupils and the wider community as active, reflective, collaborative learners. They can cope with the move towards greater inclusion because they have a shared commitment to each other's learning, and a clear understanding of where they are going. Learning communities are receptive to new ideas and they have learning-friendly inclusive cultures. The DfES (2003b) comments: 'We want to see special schools take a leading role in helping mainstream schools develop more inclusive learning environments' (DfES 2003b: para. 8).

Involving parents and carers of SEN pupils as more equal partners in the learning community is important too, and special schools working with mainstream schools can effectively support this development. A parent of a SEN child comments in the DfES report of the special schools working group, on schools as learning communities:

. . . Schools are at the heart of all our communities – but not all truly value diversity. Our main concern is for our children to have high quality well-resourced education which will lead to a valued adult life – not problem-orientated, but supportive and confident. (DfES 2003b: 126.3)

Six key features occurring concurrently, which foster inclusive learning communities have been recognised by Stoll *et al.* (2003). The key features are as follows:

1. *Community dialogue* – shared purpose about inclusion developed through ongoing dialogue between all stakeholders.
2. *Self-evaluation* – involving strategic thinking, planning and action to create useful new knowledge about inclusion, for the benefit of the school learning community.
3. *Team learning* – ongoing collective professional learning where teachers learn from and with each other in practice, i.e. special and mainstream school staff working in partnership.
4. *Re-culturing* – re-visiting and challenging cultural norms, ensuring they are supportive of collective learning, i.e. collective commitment and shared responsibility towards inclusion, a willingness to try something different, or to adopt new approaches to learning.
5. *Creativity and spontaneity* – open to new ideas, thinking 'outside the box', divergent and innovative thinking, risk-taking.
6. *Connecting all knowledge* – the 'big picture', joined-up thinking, seeing relationships, processes and patterns of change that make up the entire inclusive learning community, the ability to analyse more deeply the factors underlying the concerns and difficulties with inclusion.

Benefits and outcomes

Stoll *et al.* (2003) see ten benefits for schools becoming inclusive learning communities, particularly where special schools and mainstream schools are working in partnership.

1. *Enhanced capacity* – mainstream school can make the inclusion of more complex SEN pupils a reality because of the support, advice and guidance received from the partner special school.
2. *Adaptivity* – changes can be made to become more inclusive because of increased confidence among staff.
3. *Re-cultured* – challenged and changed inappropriate culture, ethos and beliefs replaced with norms that value and support inclusive learning.
4. *Wider choice of behaviours* – broader repertoire of how to deal with increasing diversity.
5. *Restructured* – amended and revised policies and structures in order to become more flexible.
6. *Created new knowledge* – know how to work best.
7. *Real team learning* – collective commitment to learning through openness, inclusiveness and dialogue.
8. *Community commitment* – parents and members of the local community are more willing to participate in inclusive school development.

9. *Collective focus on pupil learning* – pupils' learning experience is holistic.
10. *Ultimate improvements in pupil learning* – positive professional communities exist with teachers experiencing learning enrichment.

(Stoll *et al.* 2003: 156–8)

Principles of monitoring and evaluation

Monitoring and evaluation go together in school self-review of SEN and inclusion. Monitoring the effectiveness of provision is important for evaluating the success or otherwise of inclusive schooling. Monitoring and evaluation are closely related to accountability, which involves schools demonstrating that SEN and inclusion resources are deployed effectively, in order to maintain and improve standards.

Evaluation involves the collection, analysis, discussion and reporting of evidence, which informs judgements on the success or otherwise of policy and provision for SEN and inclusion.

Monitoring concerns checking what is happening in relation to SEN and inclusion policy and practice, and the extent to which developments have gone according to plan. In other words, have the partnership schools done what they indicated they would do in their inclusion action plans, and has this had a positive impact on SEN pupils' learning?

Monitoring is an important part of inclusion, but it is only as good as the quality of information on which it is based, and whether the monitoring system used is fair and equitable, across a range of schools.

Monitoring provides a quality assurance check; it informs future decision-making, and helps to challenge any complacency that may exist in relation to SEN and inclusion. It also acknowledges the contributions of staff from the special and the mainstream schools in implementing agreed policy and delivering good quality inclusive practice.

In addition, monitoring extends existing knowledge about access issues, and teaching and learning; it supports the extension of teachers' repertoires to meet a diversity of pupils' more complex learning needs. Monitoring helps partnership schools to identify what forms of support and development are required, in order to continue to move inclusion forward.

The two main purposes of monitoring are to provide measures of success or failure about SEN and inclusion partnership practice, and to provide feedback, to inform the review of policy and provision. Robust monitoring procedures are essential in order to ensure that:

- LEA, external support services or special school inputs have been effective in mainstream settings;
- inclusive learning has been supported effectively;
- pupils with SEN/AEN make good progress and achieve well;
- additional resources impact on raising standards.

It is essential that monitoring includes information about the process and impact of inclusion, particularly where special and mainstream schools have been involved jointly in the inclusion of dual-registered SEN pupils.

How to monitor SEN and inclusion

Supported self-review is the best way to monitor SEN and inclusion, with LEAs and schools working in partnership. Self-review provides a 'light touch' monitoring framework. It is developmental, enabling schools to reflect on and improve inclusive practice. Self-review gathers first-hand evidence which, in turn, contributes to building up a school profile on SEN and inclusion. School self-review complements other external procedures such as OFSTED inspections, and LEAs can use the information and evidence gathered to intervene in inverse proportion to success.

Special and mainstream schools, through supported self-review, can monitor and evaluate their own performance against an agreed framework of inclusion indicators, such as those produced by the DfES, OFSTED or other inclusion quality mark schemes.

The provision of monitoring information on SEN and inclusion, judged against a set of agreed criteria, will allow partner schools to base their own actions on a more consistent evidence base. Management approaches between the special and mainstream partnership schools must be flexible and adaptable enough to respond to the changes or necessary improvements required in inclusive practice, as indicated by the outcomes of the monitoring process.

Schemes such as the Inclusion Quality Mark (IQM) or the Standards for Inclusion, which link closely to the process of school improvement, play a key role in school effectiveness, and can be managed within any school's existing self-review system. They provide an excellent process for self-monitoring the development of increasingly inclusive practice. The key feature of both schemes is supported ownership and development by the school itself for self-review, with a 'critical friend' approach via external moderation. The IQM and the Standards for Inclusion provide level descriptors on what inclusive policy and practice looks like, in a range of educational settings. This enables schools to collect the necessary evidence, and make secure judgements about the quality of their inclusive practice.

Governors' monitoring role

The Audit Commission (2002a) indicated that the monitoring of SEN and inclusion by governors in schools was very variable in quality and rigour. This is largely as a result of governors, in their roles as 'critical friends', not always being provided with the necessary evidence and information about the performance of children with SEN, how resources have been deployed, and how they have impacted on pupil performance. In addition, governors' knowledge of current developments in SEN and inclusion such as the P scales, QCA EBD scales, dual placements and the partnership role of special schools, varies a great deal.

Governors need to monitor progress towards the school's Accessibility Plan as well as the Inclusion Action Plan, and in particular, how any external inputs from the partner special school have led to improvements in mainstream school inclusion and accessibility.

The following questions outlined in the Audit Commission report on SEN in mainstream schools provide a useful checklist for governors with responsibility for SEN and inclusion.

SEN pupil profile

- Number of children at Action, Action Plus and Statement.
- Number of children with different types of SEN/AEN.
- Gender and ethnic profile of children with SEN.
- Number of dual registered SEN children.

Staff skills

- When SEN and inclusion-related skills were last reviewed.
- The outcomes form an audit of mainstream staff's knowledge and skills in inclusive practice.
- What SEN and inclusion training has been undertaken, in view of including more complex SEN pupils or dual registered pupils, and what the impact on raising standards has been.

The deployment of resources

- Core budget.
- Funding for pupils with Statements/dual placements.
- Funding for SEN pupils without Statements.
- Support from external agencies, services, and partner special schools.

Accessibility

- Accessibility of school buildings, curriculum materials and general school information, and the plans to extend and improve this, as outlined in the school Accessibility Plan.
- The quality of advice, guidance and support provided by external agencies, including the partnership special school.

Outcomes

- Academic attainment, key life skills, and progress in PSHCE and behaviour, made by SEN pupils, i.e. value added rates of progress, over time, and how this compares with similar schools, or across a range of settings.
- Pupil and parental attendance at interim and annual reviews.
- Attendance of pupils with SEN – authorised and unauthorised absence.
- Exclusion rates for SEN pupils – permanent and fixed term.

(Audit Commission 2002a: 109)

Examples of a joint partnership whole-school monitoring framework for SEN and inclusion, and a partnership subject monitoring inclusion and access schedule, are illustrated on the following pages (Figures 4.1, 4.2).

Figure 4.1 Monitoring mainstream and special school inclusion links

Aspect of inclusion	Score 1–4	Evidence	Impact	Future action
Leadership and management				
Pupil progress				
Pupils' attitudes, values and personal development				
Inclusive teaching and learning				
Staff continuing professional development				
Resources for inclusion				
External partnerships (special school), external agencies				
Parent partnership				
Inclusion environment: ethos, culture and access				

(Adapted from the Standards for Inclusion and the IQM, 2002)

Scoring: 1 = pre-emergent, not yet in place;
           2 = emergent and developing;
           3 = established, embedded and securely in place;
           4 = advanced - local, regional or national recognition for excellent practice

Figure 4.2 Partnership inclusion monitoring framework: subject access

Aspect of inclusion	Score 1–4	Evidence	Impact	Future action
All subject staff understand concept and principles of inclusion, and apply these consistently				
Subject SoW and PoS indicate appropriate curriculum differentiation				
Subject teacher planning indicates appropriate curriculum access strategies				
Subject teacher planning links clearly to pupils IEPs, PSPs, ILPs				
Subject teachers understand the NC inclusion statement				
Subject teachers set suitable learning challenges				
Subject teachers respond to pupils' diverse learning needs				
Subject teachers overcome potential barriers to learning				
Subject teachers deploy additional resources effectively in lessons, e.g. TAs, ICT, outreach teachers				
Subject teachers CPD on SEN and inclusion informs and improves their teaching				
Subject teachers meet regularly with staff from the special school to share ideas on best practice				

Aspect of inclusion	Score 1–4	Evidence	Impact	Future action
Subject teachers have planned meetings with TAs to discuss pupil progress, and feed back on effectiveness of support and intervention				
Subject teachers use appropriate assessment for SEN pupils learning, which informs their planning and teaching				
Subject teachers moderate P scale and NC assessments with other colleagues from the special school, or cluster				
Subject teachers can demonstrate value added rates of progress for pupils with SEN				
Subject teachers involve SEN pupils in reviewing their own progress and provision, where appropriate				
Subject teachers apply cross-curricular skills and national strategies in their teaching				
Subject teachers employ effective and positive behaviour management strategies in lessons				
Classroom organisation promotes access to learning and participation				

Aspect of inclusion	Score 1–4	Evidence	Impact	Future action
Subject teachers employ diagnostic marking, which informs SEN pupils what they need to do in order to improve, or reach their set targets				
Subject teachers engage SEN/dual placement pupils in out-of-hours learning activities				
Inclusion features on the agendas of subject or KS strategy team meetings				
Inclusion is a priority on the subject development plan				
The subject leader reports to the governing body on the progress of inclusive policy and practice in the subject				
There is strong leadership of inclusion within the subject team				
The management of inclusion within the subject area is effective				
The monitoring and evaluation of SEN and inclusion within the subject area is rigorous, and informs future improvement				

Scoring: 1 = pre-emergent, not yet in place;
2 = emergent and developing;
3 = established, embedded and securely in place;
4 = advanced – local, regional or national recognition for excellent practice

Figure 4.3 School self-review for the inclusion of SEN pupils

The following pages provide a self-evaluation schedule, based on the revised OFSTED school inspection framework, introduced in September 2003, for reviewing the inclusion of SEN children and young people in early years settings, and in mainstream primary and secondary schools.

Schools, under the SEN Code of Practice, have a duty to fulfil specific obligations, in relation to SEN provision.

Schools therefore must fulfil their statutory duties to:

(a) use their best endeavours to secure that, if any pupil has SEN, the special educational provision which their learning difficulties call for, is made;

(b) secure that pupils' needs are made known to all who are likely to teach them;

(c) secure that the teachers in the school are aware of the importance of identifying and providing for those pupils who have SEN;

(d) that where a pupil with SEN is being educated in a mainstream school, those concerned with making special educational provision for the child shall secure that the child engages in activities of the school, together with children who do not have SEN;

(e) inform parents/carers of a decision made by the school that their child has SEN:

(f) plan, over time, to increase access to the curriculum, to premises and to information;

(g) take reasonable steps to ensure that disabled pupils or prospective pupils are not placed at a substantial disadvantage, either in relation to the admission arrangements to the school, or associated services provided by or on behalf of the school.

The purpose of this self-review document is to enable senior managers, SENCOs and the governing body to evaluate the quality of SEN policy and provision within their school, matching it against the new OFSTED criteria (introduced in September 2003), and the OFSTED quality grade descriptors.

1 Excellent	2 Very good	3 Good	4 Satisfactory	5 Unsatisfactory	6 Poor	7 Very poor
Worth disseminating outside the school	Worth disseminating within own school	Worth reinforcing and developing	Adequate, but scope for improvement	Needs attention	Needs urgent action	Immediate radical change needed

Aspect	As SENCO, how do you know?	Evidence criteria checklist
1. How successful is SEN in the school? Evaluation score =	What has improved most in SEN, since the last inspection? What still needs improvement in SEN, and what action is being taken? What do parents/carers of SEN pupils, and SEN pupils themselves like most about the school? What needs improvement, and what action is being taken?	■ No. of SEN pupils on register at each graduated response? ■ % with SEN out of total school pupil population ■ Nature, continuum of SEN diversity ■ Gender and ethnicity representation among SEN pupils ■ Strengths and weaknesses of SEN in the school, i.e. what areas of SEN do we do well and what could we do better for our SEN pupils ■ Progress made in SEN since last inspection ■ Reputation of school's SEN provision in local community
2. What must the school/department do to improve SEN Evaluation score =		■ Actions to address, arising from inspection findings ■ Actions listed in order of priority (by OFSTED).
3.1. How high are standards in SEN? (progress of SEN pupils) Evaluation score =	In which areas of learning, subjects or courses do SEN pupils do best, and why? In which areas or subjects is improvement needed, and what action is being taken?	■ Prior attainment of SEN pupils on entry, and year on year (benchmarking) ■ The 'value added' rates of progress ■ Trends over time ■ Use of SEN data and information, to inform provision, teacher planning, IEP target setting ■ How well SEN pupils achieve at each key stage and in different subjects ■ To what extent SEN pupils' basic skills, key skills enable them to progress, across the curriculum, i.e. literacy, numeracy, ICT ■ Grouping, setting arrangements – withdrawal, catch-up, inclusion opportunities ■ Levels and quality of additional support for SEN pupils
3.2 How well are SEN pupils' attitudes, values and other personal qualities developed? • Attendance punctuality of SEN pupils Evaluation score =	What most needs improvement and what action is being taken?	■ Attendance data for SEN pupils ■ How good attendance, punctuality is promoted among SEN pupils ■ Correlation between attendance and SEN pupil attainment/progress ■ How poor attendance of SEN pupils is followed up

Aspect	As SENCO, how do you know?	Evidence criteria checklist
• Attitudes, behaviour, exclusions Evaluation score =	Which are the strongest aspects, and why? What most needs improvement, and what action is being taken?	■ Monitoring of SEN pupils' behaviour in lessons, and around school ■ SEN pupils' relationships with staff, other peers ■ SEN pupils' attitudes to school, motivation and interest level in lessons ■ Self-esteem and confidence levels among SEN pupils ■ SEN pupils' independence, willingness to take responsibility ■ Staff and SEN pupils' expectations ■ Low bullying, racism, sexism in relation to SEN pupils tackled ■ Exclusion rates and SEN pupils, reasons for exclusion
• SMSC (Spiritual, moral, social and cultural development) Evaluation score =	Which are the strongest aspects, and why? What most needs improvement, and what action is being taken?	■ SEN pupils' understanding and respect for others' feelings, values, beliefs ■ SEN pupils' knowledge of right from wrong ■ SEN pupils' appreciation of cultural diversity, and world culture.
4. How effective are teaching and learning for SEN pupils? • (Teaching) Evaluation score =	Which are the strongest features of teaching SEN pupils, and why? What aspects of teaching SEN pupils most need improvement, and what action is being taken?	Do all teachers, including the SENCO: ■ Plan effectively and share clear learning objectives with SEN pupils? ■ Interest, motivate, encourage and engage SEN pupils in learning? ■ Have high expectations of SEN pupils, and challenge them appropriately? ■ Use suitable, appropriate teaching strategies, methods and resources? ■ Insist on high standards of behaviour during lessons? ■ Make effective use of TAs and other support? ■ Use homework effectively with SEN pupils to reinforce and extend their learning?
• (Learning) Evaluation score =	Which are the strongest features of learning, and why? Which aspects of learning most need improvement for SEN pupils, and what action is being taken?	■ SEN pupils acquire new knowledge, skills, develop ideas and increase understanding ■ SEN pupils show engagement, application, concentration, and are productive ■ SEN pupils develop skills and capacity to work independently and collaboratively

Aspect	As SENCO, how do you know?	Evidence criteria checklist
• The quality of assessment of SEN pupils' work	What are the strongest features of assessment for SEN pupils, and why? What aspects of SEN pupil assessment most need improvement, and what action is being taken?	The extent to which teachers: ■ assess SEN pupils' work thoroughly and constructively ■ use assessment to inform planning, target setting (on IEPs) ■ ensure SEN pupils understand how well they are doing, and how they can improve.
Evaluation score =		
5. How well does the curriculum meet SEN pupils' needs? • curriculum breadth to match SEN pupils' interests, aptitudes and needs	What are the best and most innovative parts of the curriculum for SEN pupils, and why? Which areas of the curriculum most need improvement for SEN pupils, and what action is being taken?	■ Curriculum provides well for SEN pupils, i.e. alternative, whole curriculum ■ Curriculum is inclusive, giving equality of access and opportunity for SEN pupils ■ Prepares SEN pupils for next stage/phase of education, employment, further study ■ SEN pupils do not miss any elements of curriculum e.g. RE, collective worship ■ SEN pupils gain appropriate access to PSHE, Citizenship, sex and drugs education ■ Curriculum innovation and development occurs for SEN pupils
Evaluation score =		
• opportunity for enrichment through extra-curricular provision	Which are the best features, and why? What most needs improvement, and what action is being taken?	■ Provides support for SEN pupils' learning outside school day, i.e. breakfast, homework, study support clubs ■ Provision of out-of-hours learning activities for SEN pupils – sport, art, etc.
Evaluation score =		
• quality and quantity of accommodation and resources to meet curriculum needs of SEN pupils	Which are the best features, and why? What most needs improvement, and what action is being taken?	■ Sufficient teaching and support staff with qualifications and experience to match curriculum demands for SEN pupils ■ Accommodation that allows curriculum to be taught effectively to SEN pupils ■ Sufficient resources to meet the needs of the SEN pupils and their curriculum requirements
Evaluation score =		
6. How well are SEN pupils cared for, guided and supported? • SEN pupils' care, welfare, health and safety	Which are the most effective aspects, and why? What most needs improvement, and what action is being taken?	■ Effective procedures for the protection of pupils in line with locally agreed child protection arrangements ■ SEN pupils work in a healthy and safe environment
Evaluation score =		

Aspect	As SENCO, how do you know?	Evidence criteria checklist
• provides support, advice and guidance for SEN pupils, based on the monitoring of their personal development Evaluation score =	Which are the most effective aspects of care, guidance and support, and why? What most needs improvement, and what action is being taken?	■ Each SEN pupil has a good and trusting relationship with one or more adults in the school ■ SEN pupils have access to well-informed support, advice and guidance, as they progress through the school ■ There are effective induction arrangements for SEN pupils entering the school at any point during the year ■ Secondary SEN pupils have information, impartial guidance (including Connexions personal advisers at 13–19) that are effective in leading them towards further study, appropriate career opportunities.
• seeks to involve SEN pupils in its work and development Evaluation score =	Which are the most effective aspects, and why? What most needs improvement, and what action is being taken?	■ The school seeks, values, and acts on the views of SEN pupils ■ The SEN pupils' 'voice' is heard, and they are represented on the School Council.
7. How well does the school work in partnership with parents/carers of SEN pupils, and with other schools and the community? • the effectiveness of the links with parents/carers, families of SEN pupils Evaluation score =	What are the strongest features, and why? What most needs improvement, and what action is being taken?	■ All parents/carers of SEN pupils receive appropriate information about SEN provision in the school, and general school information ■ All parents/carers of SEN pupils receive information about their child's standards and progress ■ Parents'/carers' views are sought and acted upon ■ Partnership with parents/carers contributes to SEN pupils' learning at school and at home ■ Any parental complaints or concerns regarding SEN provision, pupil progress, or behaviour, are dealt with promptly, effectively, to parents' satisfaction
• the quality of any links with the local community Evaluation score =	What are the strongest features, and why? What most needs improvement, and what action is being taken?	■ Providing a resource for, and drawing from, the community

Aspect	As SENCO, how do you know?	Evidence criteria checklist
• the effectiveness of extended school services and educational and support programmes for parents, families, community members Evaluation score =	What are the strongest features, and why? What could be improved, and what action is being taken?	■ Provision is of high quality ■ Provision meets identified needs ■ It results in educational benefits to SEN pupils at the school
• school's SEN links with other schools and colleges Evaluation score =	What are the strongest features, and why? What could be improved, and what action is being taken?	■ There is an effective mechanism for the transfer of SEN pupils ■ There is effective SEN collaboration with other schools and contribution to wider partnerships ■ There are efficient management arrangements for school or linked provision
8. How well is SEN led and managed? • SEN Governor, Governing Body Evaluation score =	What are the strongest features, and why? What could be improved, and what action is being taken?	■ SEN Governor/governing body fulfils its statutory SEN duties, including promoting SEN policy ■ Has a good understanding of the strengths and weaknesses of SEN in the school ■ Challenges and supports the SMT, in relation to SEN ■ Monitors SEN policy and provision with the SENCO ■ SEN governor is clear about their role, they analyse SEN pupil data, and judge value for money. ■ SEN governor helps shape SEN vision and direction
• the quality of leadership of SEN, particularly by the SENCO Evaluation score =	What are the key features of SEN leadership in the school? In what ways can school SEN leadership be improved, and what action is being taken?	■ There is a clear vision, sense of purpose, high aspirations and a focus on SEN pupils' achievement, conveyed to SEN team, and other staff ■ Strategic planning at whole school and department level promotes ambitions/goals for SEN ■ Staff, and SEN pupils are inspired, motivated and influenced by the SENCO's leadership ■ An effective team is created for SEN ■ SENCO demonstrates their knowledge and innovative leadership of teaching and the curriculum for SEN ■ A whole school approach to SEN and inclusion exists, which is equitable ■ SENCO provides a good role model to staff, and for SEN pupils

Aspect	As SENCO, how do you know?	Evidence criteria checklist
• the effectiveness of the management of SEN	Which aspects of managing SEN performance of the school/dept work best, and why? In what ways does the management of SEN performance need improvement, and what action is being taken? Which are the strongest features of the school's management of resources for SEN, and why? What aspects of SEN resource management need improvement, and what action is being taken?	■ There is rigorous self –evaluation of SEN undertaken, and findings are used effectively ■ SEN pupil performance data is analysed, monitored, evaluated and used to review trends/patterns, and to inform appropriate action ■ The quality of staff competence in SEN team is monitored through PMT assessment process to bring about improvement ■ The contribution of SENCO to the CPD of SEN staff, and other staff in the school on SEN ■ New members of staff to the school/SEN team are well inducted, i.e. TAs, NQTs, ITT students ■ TAs/LSAs are effectively deployed throughout the school ■ The recruitment, retention, deployment and workload of SEN staff is managed effectively ■ The management of resources for SEN (budget/funding) is well managed, to provide best value
Evaluation score =		
• the effect of any particular aids or barriers to raising SEN pupils' achievement, within school or externally	Which aids or removal of barriers have had the greatest impact on raising achievement, and why? What aspects of access for SEN pupils most need improvement, and what action is being taken?	■ The annual school access audit identifies potential barriers that require removal ■ The school's accessibility plan identifies the actions and resources required to remove potential barriers ■ ICT, multi-media, other alternative methods to recording other than writing, are utilised in lessons ■ There is full access for pupils with SEN and disability to school buildings, curriculum, out-of-hours learning activities, educational visits, and information ■ Pupils with SEN and disability have full access to community facilities used by the school ■ Pupils with SEN and disability have full access to other local partnership schools
Evaluation score =		

Aspect	As SENCO, how do you know?	Evidence criteria checklist
9. How good is the quality of education in areas of learning, subjects and courses? • for each area of learning in the Foundation Stage, and subject or course inspected in depth Evaluation score =	In which subjects, or aspects of subjects/courses do SEN pupils do best, and why? In which subjects, or aspects of subjects/courses is improvement needed, and what action is being taken?	■ The overall quality of provision, based on its effectiveness ■ The standards achieved by SEN pupils ■ The quality of inclusive teaching and learning ■ The quality of curriculum leadership ■ Any other factors that have a bearing on pupils' achievement, i.e. managing diversity and promoting equality ■ How quality and standards have changed since the last inspection, highlighting strengths and weaknesses
• work seen in other subjects and courses Evaluation score =		■ Applicable criteria from relevant parts of the OFSTED evaluation schedule
10. Quality of other specified features e.g. unit, or special class provision • what is the overall effectiveness of this provision? Evaluation score =	What are the strongest aspects of unit/special class provision, and why? What most needs improvement, and what action is being taken?	This will include: ■ the impact of the provision on SEN pupil achievement ■ the quality of what is provided ■ the effectiveness with which the unit/special class is led, managed and organised, by the teacher in charge ■ the quality and sufficiency of resources in the unit/special class ■ how well the unit provision/special class provision is monitored and evaluated

LEAs monitoring and evaluating SEN and inclusion

OFSTED LEA inspection evidence, and the Audit Commission findings (2002), indicated that barely half of LEAs knew anything about the impact of their SEN and inclusion strategy on pupils' attainment and progress, because they were not monitoring such work systematically.

Lunt, in Campbell (2002), comments on the great variation existing between educational settings, and the wide range of pupil diversity within a school, which makes monitoring and evaluating inclusion so variable. Caution needs to be exercised in measuring inclusive schooling, particularly in relation to the tensions that exist between processes and outcomes. The best approach to adopt is one that demonstrates what works in inclusive education.

LEAs, in partnership with schools, through a process of supported self-review, will be able to:

■ develop more robust, but open monitoring systems, to assess if inclusion provision adds value;
■ clarify each other's role in monitoring inclusion performance;
■ specify what difference their inclusion provision makes to pupils' progress and attainment;
■ become more effective in sustaining continuous school improvement; and
■ develop more consistent inclusion policy, practice and provision, within schools, across the LEA.

LEAs and schools will need to monitor the following aspects of SEN and inclusion:

■ implementation of the NC inclusion statement;
■ fulfilling statutory duties for SEN and disability;
■ policy reflecting inclusive practice;
■ standards of attainment among different groups of pupils or individual dual registered SEN pupils;
■ resources, funding and value for money, best value and added value;
■ effectiveness of identification, and the procedures for those who experience barriers to learning and participation;
■ quality of teaching and learning;
■ leadership and management of SEN and inclusion;
■ effectiveness and impact of additional resources;
■ exclusion and unauthorised absence rates among SEN pupils;
■ level of satisfaction among parents/carers and SEN pupils.

Through the monitoring process, LEAs will gain greater oversight of the standards of inclusion existing in their schools. This will also provide a secure evidence base for agreed triggers for LEA intervention, where SEN/AEN pupils are not making reasonable or adequate progress, or where parents/carers have repeated concerns about provision.

Monitoring the effectiveness of provision, including the value added and cost effectiveness, is vital for evaluating the inclusion process, and providing evidence to underpin LEA SEN and inclusion policy and strategy. Lunt, in Campbell (2002) comments:

. . . the absence of strong evidence for the superiority of segregated special schooling gives encouragement to policies which include a wider diversity of SEN in mainstream schools. (Campbell 2002: 49)

The Audit Commission report (2002a) commented:

Comparative information on the performance of pupils with similar levels of need, across different schools or over time, could throw light on which pupils are making good progress and which are falling behind. This could help schools to review their own practice and enable the LEA to target its advice and support more effectively. (Audit Commission 2002a: 114)

LEAs need to strengthen the links between their SEN services and the school improvement service, of inspectors and advisers by:

- further developing link advisers and school improvement officers expertise in relation to SEN and inclusion; and
- the collection and analysis of SEN pupil performance data, including those in special schools. This should form a key element of school self-review.

Both SEN services and school improvement services need to share information and work together, in order to support continuous improvement in inclusion and SEN provision. This joint working can help to inform the LEA process of categorisation of schools, which will have SEN and inclusion as one of its performance indicators.

An outcome of LEA monitoring and evaluation of SEN and inclusion within its schools should inform the answers to the following questions.

- To what extent has there been a change and improvement in the commitment of schools to become more inclusive in their ways of working?
- To what extent has the concept of identifying and removing barriers to inclusion been embedded into schools' inclusion policy and practice?
- To what extent did the partnership working between mainstream and special schools contribute to more inclusive collaborative ways of working?
- Who else could contribute in future years to moving inclusive partnership practice forward?
- To what extent were inclusion priorities identified, that could have been overlooked?
- Were appropriate information-gathering methods utilised, and could these be improved?
- How might the SEN and inclusion process be improved?

(McDonald and Olley 2002: 32–3)

LEA inclusion strategy

According to the Audit Commission report on SEN in mainstream schools (2002a), the LEA inclusion strategy should:

- be 'needs based', i.e. based on the analysis of current SEN pupils' high support needs, and on needs profiles for the next five to ten years, with a

view to including them in mainstream schools, where appropriate and practicable;
■ set out a timetable for developing the capacity of mainstream schools and early years settings, to include SEN pupils with more complex needs, from the special school sector; and
■ specify the future role of special schools.

LEAs are expected to support, empower and challenge their schools to become more inclusive. They also need to be open about their plans to develop inclusion, and the future role of special schools.

LEAs will be more inclined to listen to special schools if they have established themselves as a credible source of expertise. Varying practice exists among LEAs, and the future role of special schools is very much dependent on the political 'will' and context existing within the local area. There is still a lack of clarity in relation to national inclusion guidance, expectations and targets, for LEAs.

The LEA strategy for inclusion should set out clearly the future role of special schools in the spectrum of provision, and indicate how this is to be achieved.

The LEA will need to consider the changing profile of the special school population and the implications for training and capital developments; their recruitment and retention strategy; the promotion of partnership working between special and mainstream schools; the further inclusion of special school children in mainstream settings; and the reduction of surplus special school places. The Audit Commission (2002a) recommends the following:

■ LEAs should promote partnership working between mainstream and special schools, to make the most of specialist expertise, and to create opportunities for children in special schools, to spend time learning alongside their mainstream peers.
■ LEAs should consider the scope for developing local special schools to provide advice and support to their mainstream counterparts.
■ LEAs should develop the training role of special schools where they have relevant expertise – both in terms of outreach work and on-site training – as well as fostering learning opportunities between mainstream and special schools.

In a later report, the Audit Commission considered the monitoring and evaluation of the impact of schools' work on SEN and inclusion to be a key responsibility for LEAs. In particular, LEAs need to map out the role currently played by mainstream schools, mainstream resourced provision and special schools, with a view to considering the scope for further inclusion in mainstream settings, of SEN pupils from the special school sector.

Inclusion is unlikely to be achieved either rapidly or 'on the cheap'. Rather, the integration of pupils with higher levels of needs and the redevelopment of special schools will require careful planning and targeted investment over a number of years. In the short to medium term, this may involve 'double running-costs', for example, when developing new provision while maintaining a special school. (Audit Commission 2002b: 38)

The same report goes on to state:

Special schools have much potential to support mainstream schools in responding to some children's needs as has been demonstrated by successful outreach arrangements in a number of areas. This may involve staff training initiatives or information sharing on effective strategies for working with children with particular needs. LEAs should explore the scope for developing their special schools, where appropriate, as resource centres to support their mainstream counterparts. (Audit Commission 2002b: 70)

Illustrated below (Figure 4.4) are selected extracts from the Audit Commission's checklists for LEAs, on developing the capacity of schools and early years settings to become more inclusive, which relate to the role of special schools.

Figure 4.4 Checklist for LEAs on developing the capacity of schools to become more inclusive

	Action required
Do the LEAs funding arrangements promote inclusive practice by: ■ encouraging mainstream schools to admit and retain children with high levels of need, or challenging behaviour? ■ encouraging special schools to enable pupils to take part in some mainstream school activities? ■ encouraging schools (special and mainstream) to work together to share their skills and experience on SEN? **Accessing specialist expertise** ■ What scope is there for developing outreach so that special school staff can advise and support their mainstream colleagues? ■ Has the LEA sought to develop the training role of special schools where they have the relevant expertise – both in terms of outreach work and on-site training – and to foster learning opportunities between mainstream and special schools? ■ Are there plans to re-distribute resources and staff expertise to pursue the inclusion strategy? (Audit Commission 2002b: 37–9)	

Appendix 1:
Inclusive learning services marketing brochure

Leafy Lane School

Introduction

Leafy Lane School is a special school with a resource and information centre, in addition to operating a high quality inclusion outreach service. The school caters for children and young people from Foundation Stage up to Key Stage 4 with moderate and severe learning difficulties, who may also have accompanying low incidence, additional educational needs such as speech and language difficulties or autistic spectrum disorders.

The school Inclusion Team, ably led by the Inclusion Manager, provides advice, guidance, support and targeted intervention for any pupils undertaking mainstream school inclusion experiences, or who are dual registered.

The school has an excellent reputation, and its credibility has been recognised through the following awards and achievements:

- DfEE Excellence Award in 2001
- Beacon Status in 2002
- Training school for ITT and NQTs in 2003
- Investors in People in 2003
- Inclusion Quality Mark in 2004
- Application for the Extended School Programme, and awaiting outcome
- Leading Literacy and Numeracy Teachers
- Two Advanced Skills Teachers: one in ICT and the other for Inclusion.

How to obtain inclusion services

Referral can come from the LEA, following the outcome from a statement review or a statutory assessment, particularly in the case of dual registered pupils.
Mainstream schools within the public and private sector, can purchase inclusion services via Service Level Agreements, or on a 'pay as you use' basis.

SEN AND INCLUSION TRAINING
Training school for ITT and NQTs.
Customised INSET on SEN, disability
access and inclusive learning.
Coaching and mentoring.

ASSESSMENT
Assessment placements.
Using data to inform planning,
teaching and IEP target setting.
Moderation of P scales.

OUTREACH SERVICE
Early Years to KS4.
High quality in-class support.
Team teaching.
Curriculum differentiation.
Consultancy and advice.

OTHER INCLUSION SERVICES
SENCO/INCO Networks.
Curriculum resource loan services.
Disability access advice service.
Demonstration lessons.
Parent advice centre and workshops.

Appendix 2: Inclusion service level agreement

Leafy Lane School Inclusion Service

Meeting the needs of children with severe and moderate learning difficulties

Three inclusion packages tailored to meet your school's needs.

Basic inclusion package (Bronze)
Curriculum differentiation guidance.
Assessment guidance.
Loan of curriculum resources.

Cost: £500
Provides four half-days guidance and loan of resources.

Intermediate inclusion package (Silver)
Includes all the Basic (Bronze) package plus:
INSET
Parent Advice and Parent Workshops
Consultancy and advice on inclusion

Cost: £1,000
Provides the school with eight half-days.

Advanced inclusion package (Gold)
Includes the Basic (Bronze) and Intermediate (Silver) packages plus:
Assessment placements
Team teaching
Demonstration lessons
In-class support

Cost: £3,000
Provides the school with 16 half-days or eight full days.

SERVICE LEVEL AGREEMENT

Sign up for:	Days	Price
☐ Basic (Bronze) inclusion package		
☐ Intermediate (Silver) inclusion package		
☐ Advanced (Gold) inclusion package		

Name: _____
Address: _____
_____
Phone: _____

Method of payment:
☐ Cheque
☐ Invoice the school
☐ Direct debit from school budget

Signature: _____

Leafy Lane School Inclusion Service
Leafy Lane
Oakfield Park
Sunny Town
SU2 3ZX

Phone: 321 456 7899
Fax: 321 456 7865
E-mail: leafylane@school.com

Appendix 3:
Inclusion service
client satisfaction survey

LEAFY LANE SCHOOL INCLUSION SERVICE –
CLIENT SATISFACTION SURVEY

Using the scale below, insert a number in the relevant box, to rate the quality of provision received from the Leafy Lane Inclusion Service.

1 = poor   2 = satisfactory   3 = good

1. Impact on SEN pupils' learning ☐

2. Access to the mainstream curriculum ☐

3. Outreach in-class support ☐

4. Guidance on assessment, using the P scales and target setting ☐

5. Demonstration lessons ☐

6. Advice, guidance and consultancy offered by Inclusion Team staff ☐

7. Loan of curriculum resources and equipment hire ☐

8. SEN and disability and inclusion INSET ☐

9. Support for out-of-hours learning activities ☐

10. Workshops and Networks ☐

11. Information guides on inclusion for staff, pupils, parents, governors ☐

12. Dual registration guidance and coordination ☐

13. Parental advice and liaison ☐

14. Twenty-four-hour e-mail conferencing and telephone help line ☐

15. Inclusion website and related links ☐

16. Service Level Agreement selected: Bronze ☐   Silver ☐   Gold ☐

17. Speed of response to queries, or requests for inputs and services ☐

How could the Leafy Lane School Inclusion Service be further improved?

Thank you for taking the time to complete this survey. Please return to Leafy Lane School, within the week

Appendix 4:
Example of a special school inclusion open day programme

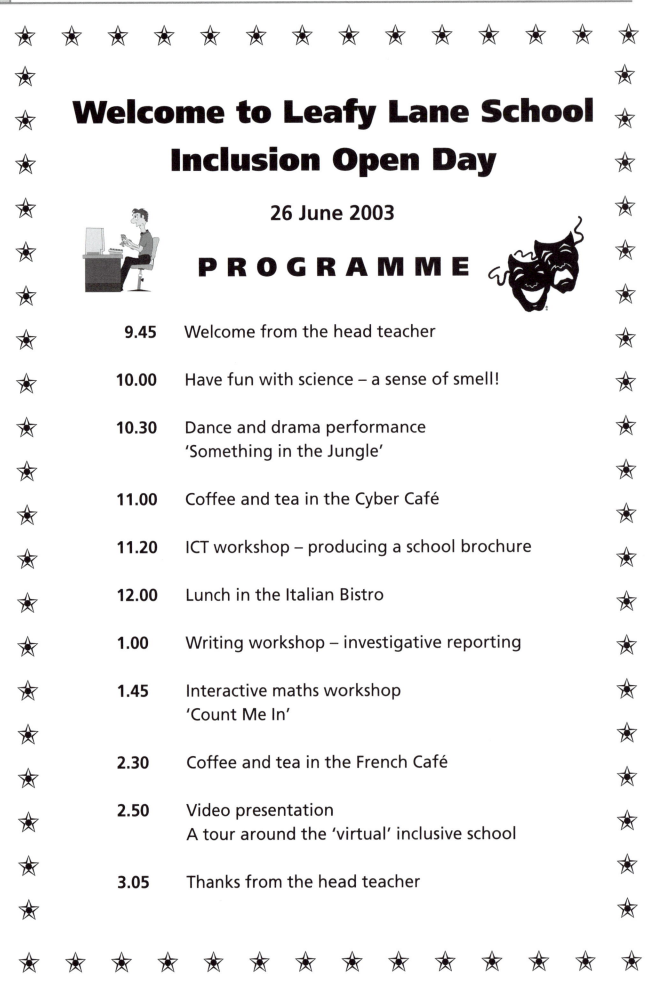

Welcome to Leafy Lane School Inclusion Open Day

26 June 2003

PROGRAMME

9.45	Welcome from the head teacher
10.00	Have fun with science – a sense of smell!
10.30	Dance and drama performance 'Something in the Jungle'
11.00	Coffee and tea in the Cyber Café
11.20	ICT workshop – producing a school brochure
12.00	Lunch in the Italian Bistro
1.00	Writing workshop – investigative reporting
1.45	Interactive maths workshop 'Count Me In'
2.30	Coffee and tea in the French Café
2.50	Video presentation A tour around the 'virtual' inclusive school
3.05	Thanks from the head teacher

Appendix 5:
Parents' and carers' guide to dual placements

A PARENTS' AND CARERS' GUIDE

TO DUAL PLACEMENTS

Contents

Introduction

What are dual placements?

Which children have dual placements?

What are the advantages of a dual placement?

What additional support do dual placements bring?

How will I know if my child is benefiting from a dual placement?

Who can I contact at school about dual placements?

Where can I find out more about dual placements?

Introduction

Welcome to the Leafy Lane and Waterfall Community School Parents' and Carers' Guide to Dual Placements. This guide has been produced as a result of both schools' Parent and Teacher Associations joining together, to decide what information should be included.

This guide will inform you about the benefits of dual placements, and how they can help your child to reach their optimum potential, in two school settings. It also tells you who you can contact if you have any further queries, or require more information about dual placements.

Parents and carers are viewed as important partners, working in collaboration with the special and mainstream school, in order to ensure that their child's dual placement is a successful and enjoyable learning experience.

This guide is available in Bengali, Gujerati, Hindi, Punjabi, Urdu and Chinese. In addition, an audio tape version can be obtained from the school, on request. You may wish to purchase or loan a copy of the Inclusion and Dual Placements video, which accompanies this guide. Copies of this video can be obtained directly from either school office.

What are dual placements?

Dual placements are where a special school child spends 51 per cent or more of their time per week being educated in a mainstream school, preferably within their local neighbourhood community

Which children have dual placements?

A child from a special school, with a statement of special educational needs, is eligible for a dual placement. The child is selected on the basis that they have made sufficient progress in their learning, personal, social, emotional and behavioural development, and are therefore ready to cope in a larger school community,

Alternatively, children who are at Action Plus or have a statement of special educational needs within a mainstream school may benefit from a dual placement each week, spending some time in a special school setting.

What are the advantages of a dual placement?

They offer your child:

- Greater opportunities to increase their circle of friends.
- Enhanced curriculum access and a wider choice of out-of-hours learning activities.
- Opportunity to experience working in a larger or smaller learning community.
- The continuance of specialist therapies in a specialist setting.
- A greater say in the level of support they require across the two school settings.
- Programmes of study tailored to meet their needs.

- A high level of pastoral care to build their confidence, develop their independence and enhance their self-esteem.

What additional support do dual placements bring?

A dual placement will bring a Learning Support Assistant (LSA) from the special school, to support your child in the mainstream setting.

If your child is a mainstream pupil with a Statement or at Action Plus they will receive additional ISA support within the special school.

A teacher from the outreach team in the special school will liaise regularly and coordinate provision with the Inclusion Coordinator in the mainstream school.

Any specialist aids or equipment will be made available in both settings in order to ensure your child can access the curriculum.

Your child will be provided with a 'pupil buddy' in either school setting.

How will I know if my child is benefiting from a dual placement?

Their self-confidence will increase.

They will be reaching their optimum potential in both school settings.

Their contributions will be valued.

They will be welcomed and accepted as members of a local learning community.

They will feel less isolated.

Who can I contact at school about dual placements?

Leafy Lane Inclusion Manager: Mrs Leach.

Waterfall Community School Inclusion Coordinator: Mr Ironside.

Both school websites provide further information via a password protected link, which guarantees confidentiality. www.leafylane/inclusion/co.uk www.waterfallsch/dualplacements/inclusion.co.uk

There is also a telephone help line for each school:

Leafy Lane School; 01562 99816 Waterfall Community School: 01531 66729.

You can also contact each school via their e-mail address:

leafylane@school.com

waterfallcommunity@school.com

Where can I find out more about dual placements?

DfES: Report of the Special School Working Group.

DfES: Inclusive Schooling: Children with special educational needs.

LEA SEN Officer: Mrs Watson.

Adviser for Inclusive Education: Mr Gill.

Parent Partnership Coordinator: Miss Finn.

Appendix 6:
The teachers' professional learning framework

These descriptors support the Performance Management Threshold Assessment process, the NQT induction procedures, and the ongoing professional development of any teacher, at any stage of their teaching career, working in special and mainstream school settings, PRUs, as well as those teachers working in support services. They can be achieved over any agreed period of time.

(When each descriptor has been met, put a tick in the box, and record the date achieved)

1. Professional learning entitlement

Date achieved

☐   Engage in sustained reflection and structured learning   _____

☐   Create learning opportunities from everyday practice, i.e.
     planning and assessing for learning   _____

☐   Ability to identify own learning and development needs, and
     those of others   _____

☐   Develop an individual professional learning plan   _____

☐   Recognise for accreditation school-based learning, as well as
     course participation   _____

☐   Develop self-evaluation, observation and peer review skills   _____

☐   Develop mentoring and coaching skills and offer professional
     dialogue and feedback   _____

☐   Plan longer-term career aspirations   _____

2. Professional learning supporting teachers' practice

☐   Reflecting on and enhancing practice   _____

☐   Identifying and addressing areas of pupil underachievement   _____

☐   Career development   _____

☐   Working with evidence to exercise creativity and judgement   _____

☐   Discovering, evaluating and embedding effective new
     approaches to teaching and learning, planning, assessment
     and the curriculum   _____

☐   Exploiting all opportunities to learn from other teachers   _____

☐ Producing, interpreting and managing classroom and pupil data   _____

☐ Developing team working   _____

☐ Developing behaviour management strategies   _____

☐ Promoting inclusion   _____

☐ Discovering the further potential of ICT for pupil and teacher learning   _____

☐ Recognising improvements in own practice   _____

3. Supports for professional learning

☐ Working within a learning team, i.e. department, Key Stage, or cross-school   _____

☐ Working with a mentor or coach   _____

☐ Collaborative teaching, planning and assessment   _____

☐ Planning, study and evaluation of lessons and other learning experiences with colleagues   _____

☐ Observing colleagues teaching   _____

☐ Sharing teaching approaches with teachers from other schools   _____

☐ Active participation in self-evaluation processes   _____

☐ Engaging in peer review   _____

☐ Collecting, interpreting and applying pupil feedback, data and outcomes   _____

☐ Observing and analysing children's responses to learning activities   _____

☐ Developing resources and projects with colleagues   _____

☐ Participating in collaborative enquiry and problem-solving   _____

☐ Leading or contributing to staff meetings and INSET   _____

☐ Engaging with subject or specialist associations, e.g. NASEN   _____

☐ Reading educational, academic and professional journals and texts   _____

☐ Participating in courses, online learning opportunities and higher education study   _____

☐ Accessing NCSL programmes   _____

☐ Taking secondments and sabbaticals   _____

4. External opportunities to share and develop professional practice

- ☐ Working across phase or within a cluster/consortium/ partnership/network on common research or development work _____

- ☐ Taking part in local, national or international teaching exchanges _____

- ☐ Undertaking development with higher education partners _____

- ☐ Networked Learning Communities _____

- ☐ Contributing to workshops, conferences and seminars _____

- ☐ Being a member of a subject, specialist or teaching association _____

- ☐ Participating in local and national steering or working groups _____

- ☐ Leading or contributing to running professional development courses _____

- ☐ Developing or moderating examinations or tests with boards _____

- ☐ Participating in national and local policy development _____

- ☐ Developing, testing and publishing materials and resources _____

- ☐ Participating in professional online communities _____

(Adapted from the General Teaching Council's Teachers' Professional Learning Framework (2003))

References and further reading

Ainscow, M., Farrell, P., Tweddle, D. and Malki, G. (1999) *Effective Practice in Inclusion and in Special and Mainstream Schools Working Together*. London: DfEE.

Audit Commission (2002a) *Special Educational Needs: A Mainstream Issue*. London: Audit Commission.

Audit Commission (2002b) *Managing Special Educational Needs: A Self-review Handbook for Local Education Authorities*. London: Audit Commission.

Birmingham Inclusion Consultancy Service (2002) *Standards for Inclusion: Self-Monitoring for School Improvement*. Birmingham: Birmingham City Council.

Blandford, S. (1997) *Middle Management in Schools: How to Harmonise Managing and Teaching for an Effective School*. London: Pearson Education.

Booth, T. and Ainscow, M. (2002) *Index for Inclusion: Developing Learning and Participation in Schools*. Bristol: CSIE.

Busher, H., Harris, A., and Wise, C. (2000) *Subject Leadership and School Improvement*. London: Paul Chapman Publishing.

Campbell, C. (2002) *Developing Inclusive Schooling: Perspectives, Policies and Practices*. London: Institute of Education, University of London.

CSIE (2002) *Inclusion Information Guide*. Bristol: Centre for Studies on Inclusive Education.

CIM (2003) *Information for Marketing*. Maidenhead: Chartered Institute of Marketing.

Coles, C. and Hancock, R. (2002) *The Inclusion Quality Mark*. Altrincham: Public Sector Matters.

Davies, B. and Ellison, L. (1996) *Strategic Marketing for Schools: How to Integrate Marketing and Strategic Development for an Effective School*. London: Pearson Education.

DfEE (1997) *Excellence for All Children: Meeting Special Educational Needs*. London: Department for Education and Employment.

DfEE (1998) *Meeting Special Educational Needs: A Programme of Action*. London: Department for Education and Employment.

DfES (2001a) *Inclusive Schooling: Children with Special Educational Needs*. London: Department for Education and Skills.

DfES (2001b) *Special Educational Needs Code of Practice*. London: Department for Education and Skills.

DfES (2002) *Including All Children in the Literacy Hour and Daily Mathematics Lesson: Management Guide*. London: Department for Education and Skills.

DfES (2003a) *SEN Action Programme*. London: Department for Education and Skills.

DfES (2003b) *The Report of the Special Schools Working Group*. London: Department for Education and Skills.

DfES (2003c) *Excellence and Enjoyment: A Strategy for Primary Schools*. London: Department for Education and Skills.

Dyson, A. and Gains, C. (1993) *Rethinking Special Needs in Mainstream Schools: Towards the Year 2000*. London: David Fulton Publishers.

Fidler, B. (2002) *Strategic Management for School Development. Leading Your School's Improvement Strategy*. London: Paul Chapman Publishing.

Fletcher-Campbell, F. and Kington, A. (2000) 'Links between special schools and mainstream schools: a follow-up survey', *Journal of Research in Special Educational Needs* 1(3).

Frost, D., Durrant, J., Head, M. and Holden, G. (2000) *Teacher-Led School Improvement.* London: Routledge Falmer.

Fullan, M. (2002) *Leading in a Culture of Change.* London: Leannta Education Associations.

GTC (2003) *The Teachers' Professional Learning Framework.* London: General Teaching Council.

Guiney, E. (2001) *Coaching Isn't Just For Athletes: The Role of Teacher Leaders.* Boston: Phi Delta Kappa International.

Jenkinson, J. C. (1997) *Mainstream or Special? Educating Students with Disabilities.* London: Routledge.

Jones, F., Jones, K. and Szwed, C. (2001) *The SENCO as Teacher and Manager: A Guide for Practitioners and Trainers.* London: David Fulton Publishers.

Jordan, L. and Goodey, C. (2002) *Human Rights and School Change: The Newham Story.* Bristol: CSIE.

Lindsay, G. (2003) 'Inclusive education: a critical perspective', *British Journal of Special Education* 30(1), 3–10.

Lunt, I., Evans, J., Norwich, B. and Wedell, K. (1994) 'Collaborating to meet special educational needs: Effective clusters?', *Support for Learning* 9(2), 73–8.

Lunt, I. And Norwich, B. (1999) *Can Effective Schools Be Inclusive Schools?* London: Institute of Education, University of London.

McDonald, V. and Olley, D. (2002) *Aspiring to Inclusion: A Handbook for Councils and Organisations.* Ipswich: Suffolk County Council.

NCSL (2003) *Leadership and Inclusion: A Special School Perspective.* Nottingham: National College for School Leadership.

OFSTED (2002) *Schools' Use of Temporary Teachers.* London: Office for Standards in Education.

OFSTED (2003a) *Annual Report of Her Majesty's Chief Inspector of Schools: Standards and Quality in Education 2001/2002.* London: Office for Standards in Education.

OFSTED (2003b) *Inspecting Schools. The Framework for Inspecting Schools in England from September 2003.* London: Office for Standards in Education.

QCA (2001) *Planning, Teaching and Assessing the Curriculum for Pupils with Learning Difficulties: General Guidelines.* London: Qualifications and Curriculum Authority.

Rose, R. and Coles, C. (2002a) 'Special and mainstream school collaboration for the promotion of inclusion', *Journal of Research in Special Educational Needs* 2(2).

Rose, R. and Coles, C. (2002b) 'A new role for special schools', *Special Children* 148, 14–16.

SCF (1997) *Towards Inclusion: SCF UK's Experience in Integrated Education.* London: Save the Children Fund.

SEED (2001) *Interchange 66: Developments in Inclusive Schooling.* Edinburgh: Scottish Executive Education Department.

Stoll, L., Fink, D. and Earl, L. (2003) *It's About Learning (and It's About Time): What's in it for Schools?* London: Routledge Falmer.

Thomas, G., Walker, D. and Webb, J. (1998) *The Making of the Inclusive School.* London: Routledge.

Tilstone, C., Florian, L. and Rose, R. (1998) *Promoting Inclusive Practice.* London: Routledge.

Tilstone, C. and Rose, R. (2002) *Strategies to Promote Inclusive Practice.* London: Routledge Falmer.

TTA (1999) *National Special Educational Needs Specialist Standards.* London: Teacher Training Agency.

Williams, S., Macalpine, A. and McCall, C. (2001) *Leading and Managing Staff Through Challenging Times.* London: The Stationery Office.

Index

Figures are in *italics*. Main mentions are in
bold.

Access factors 34
Action planning, for inclusion 16, *17*
Activities, examples of 10
Ainscow, M., DfEE research report 2–3
Audit Commission Report on SEN 4
  LEA inclusion strategy 71–3
  monitoring by governors 56–7
Audit tools 22, 41

'Buddy' schemes 10, 33

Children *see* Pupils
Classroom practice, inclusive checklist
    49–50
Clusters 52
Coaching 23–4
Code of Practice (SEN) 5
Communication competences, by special
    school outreach team 25–6
Consultancy role, of special schools 22–3
Contracts, inclusion 36, *38, 39*
CPD *see* Training

DfEE Green Paper (1997) 2
DfES definition of inclusion 3
DfES *Inclusive Schooling: Children with*
    Special Educational Needs 7
DfES Special Schools Working Group
    Report 4, 5, 23
Dual placements 3, 44, 47–8
Dual registration *see* Dual placements

Effectiveness 12–13
  special school teacher expertise 23
Evaluation 11, **55–7**
  by LEAs 70–1
  self-evaluation schedule *62–9*

Federations 53
'Full service schools' 4
Funding 3
  dual placements 47

General Teaching Council (GTC)
  Teachers' Professional Learning Frame-
    work 27, 41–2
Good practice 2, 4, **14**
Governors, monitoring role 56–7
Green Paper (DfEE 1997) 2

Inclusion
  factors for success 13
  preparation for 35–6, *37*
Inclusion facilitator, role specification *30*
Inclusion indicators (DfES) 11–12
Inclusion Quality Mark (IQM) 11, 22, **56**
Inclusion strategy, LEAs' 71–3
Inclusive learning communities 53–4
  benefits 54–5
Inclusive Learning Contracts 36, *39*
Inclusive learning plan *40*
Inclusive Schooling: Children with Special
    Educational Needs (DfES) 7
Index for Inclusion 22

Learning communities 53–4
  benefits 54–5
Learning contracts 36, *39*
Learning plan *40*
LEAs
  evaluation and monitoring 70–1
  inclusion strategy 71–3

Mainstream partnerships
  development of 5–6
  examples of development methods 9
  identification of 8, 10
Mainstream schools, contribution 34–5
Mainstream teachers
  attitudes 8
  training 36, 41–2
Management 12
Marketing, special schools 16, 18–19, *20*
Monitoring 11, **55–7**, *58–61*
  by LEAs 70–1

National Policy Board for Educational
    Administration (NPBEA)
  presentations 26

National SEN Specialist Standards **22**, *28–9*, 42, *43*, 44, *45–6*
Networks 52–3

OFSTED
 reports (2001–2) 7
 temporary teachers 41
Outcomes 11
 see also Evaluation
Outreach role, of special schools 22–3
Outreach team 24–7

Parents/carers
 dual placements 47
 learning communities 53–4
Partners, identification of 8, 10
Partnership factors
 inhibitors 35
 for successful inclusion 32–3
 in working together 8–9
Partnerships 5–6
 benefits 54–5
 inhibitors 35
 mainstream school contribution 34–5
 senior staff ix
 special school leaders role 6–7
 special schools contribution **2–8**, 9, 13
Planning *see* Action planning
Pre-inclusion checklist *37*
Preparation for inclusion 35–6
Presentations 26
Problem-solving, by special school
  outreach team 25
Programme of Action (DfEE 1998) 2
Pupil Level Annual Schools Census
  (PLASC) 11
Pupils
 achievements, recognition of 11
 learning communities 53
 learning contracts *39*
 learning plans *40*
 needs, from mainstream schools 33
 views, dual placements 47–8

Quality Mark, Inclusion (IQM) 11, 22, 56

Reports
 Ainscow, M., DfEE research 2–3
 Audit Commission on SEN 4, 56–7,
  71–3
 Chief HMI (2001–2) 3
 DfEE Green Paper (1997) 2
 DfEE *Programme of Action* (1998) 2
 DfES *Inclusive Schooling: Children with
  Special Educational Needs* 7

DfES Special Schools Working Group 4,
  5, 23
 OFSTED (2001–2) 7
 OFSTED temporary teachers 41

School self-review *62–9*
 see also Monitoring
SEN *Code of Practice* 5
SEN Specialist Standards, National 22,
  28–9, 42, *43*, 44, *45–6*
Special school head teachers, role specification *30*
Special school leaders, role in partnerships
  6–7
Special school outreach team
 communication competences 25–6
 problem-solving 25
stress management 26–7
Special schools
 coaches 23–4
 consultancy role 22–3
 inclusive practices 7, 12
 marketing 16, 18–19, *20*
 outreach role 22–3
 partnerships with mainstream schools
  ix, 6–8
  difficulties 3, 35
  examples 9
 qualities 4–5
 teacher expertise 23
 team building 24–5
 training roles 21–2
Special Schools Working Group Report
  (DfES) 23
Staff development *see* Training
Stress management, special school
  outreach team 26–7
Supply teachers 41

Teachers' Professional Learning Framework
  (TPLF)
  (GTC) 27, 41–2
Team building 24–5
Team work 24–5
Temporary teachers 41
Training
 needs 36, 41–2, *43*, 44, *45–6*
 outreach work 22–7
 provision by special schools 21–2
TTA National SEN Specialist Standards
  (1999) 22, *28–9*, 42, *43*, 44, *45–6*

'Virtual networks' 53